THE HERMITAGE WITHIN

Spirituality of the Desert

THE HERMITAGE WITHIN

WITHIN

Spirituality of the Desert

BY A MONK

Translated by Alan Neame

PAULIST PRESS • *New York/Ramsey*

Copyright © 1977 by Darton, Longman and Todd, Ltd., London. Originally published as *L'Ermitage* by Librairie Claude Martingay, Geneva, Switzerland.

Published in the United States in 1982 by Paulist Press, 545 Island Road, Ramsey, N.J. 07446.

Nihil Obstat: Fr. Dominique de Ligondes, OCR
            Fr. Jean de la Croix Bouton, OCR
Imprimi Potest: Fr. M. Ignace Gillet
            Abbot General, OCR

Library of Congress Catalog Card Number: 82-80159

ISBN: 0-8091-2428-9

Printed and bound in the United States of America

Contents

'Far away would I fly
and make a new home in the wilds.'

Psalm 55:7

'He turns her desert into an Eden,
her wasteland into the garden of Yahweh . . . '

Isaiah 51:3

'Living in the desert does not only mean
living without people, but living with God and for God.'

Serge Boulgakov

Publisher's Foreword

When self-advertisement is all the rage, here is a book by a man who will not divulge his name. Tempted as we are to thousands on thousands of external, worldly activities, here we have a book devoted to the innermost activities of the soul. Our wills daily threatened with dissolution in the shifting sands of social relationships, here we have a book about the eremitical life.

It is not enough now, if indeed it ever was, to be active in this place or that in God's name. No, we have to be active in God himself as somewhere different from everywhere else, if we really mean to follow the royal road. We have forgotten that 'God alone is good' (Lk 18:19).

Besides, as the contemplatives' memorandum to the First Episcopal Synod admirably puts it, if the hermit 'withdraws from the world, he is not deserting either it or his fellow-men; he is still entirely rooted on earth where he was born, to the resources of which he is the heir and the preoccupations and aspirations of which he does his best to make his own. No indeed, he withdraws, the better to contemplate that divine source from which the forces impelling the world forward derive their origin, and by this light the better to understand mankind's own grand designs. The desert in fact is where the soul often finds its deepest inspiration. There it was that God fashioned his people, there he took them back after their wrong-doing, "to lure them away and speak to their hearts" (Ho 2:16). There too, having overcome Satan, the Lord Jesus evinced his full power, prefiguring his Easter victory. And aren't the People of God to be reborn and renewed by a similar experience, generation by generation?'

And then, as the author of *The Hermitage Within* warns me, 'Not everyone, obviously, can and should live as a monk or hermit. But no Christian can do without an inner hermitage in which to meet his God.'

Cum quo enim Deus est,
nunquam minus solus est
quam cum solus est.

Tunc enim libere fruitur gaudio suo,
tunc ipse suus est sibi
ad fruendum Deo in se
et se in Deo . . .

He with whom God is
is never less alone
than when he is alone.

For then he can enjoy his joy,
then he is his own
to enjoy God in himself
and himself in God.

William of Saint-Thierry

Part One

THE DESERT

'I am going to lure them away,
lead them into the desert
and speak to their hearts (1).'

God is bestowing a special favour on you by drawing you into the desert. The call is a matter of God's free choice; you will only be able to persevere in it by his condescension. You will always remember how privileged you are that God should love your soul, and as time goes by you will appreciate this all the more. At the outset, inspite of what you have read and what you call your experience, you will not know what the loneliness of the desert has in store for you.

There, as elsewhere, no two souls follow precisely the same path, and God never repeats himself in his creatures. Very rarely, if at all, does he reveal his designs in advance.

Humble and detached, go into the desert. For God, awaiting you there, you bring nothing worth having, except your entire availability. The lighter your human baggage is, the poorer you will be in what the world esteems, and the greater will be your chances of success, since God will be all the freer to use you. He is calling you to live on friendly terms with him: to nothing else.

To influence others directly, even by the pen, is not one of the pursuits envisaged for the desert. You must be content to lose yourself entirely. If you secretly desire to be or to become 'somebody', you are doomed to failure. The desert is pitiless; it infallibly rejects all self-seekers.

Let us go in, in holy nakedness . . .

1. The Wilderness of the Exodus

Absence from the world

'He led his people across the desert,
for his kindness is everlasting (1).'

Going into the desert is always a solemn moment. You leave the ordinary world of social relationships for the unknown one of solitude.
Beginning involves a wrench, a break, perhaps a repudiation. The
total, final break with all that we hold dear is not achieved without
tears. It was not easy for the Hebrews to leave Egypt and they suffered for a long time afterwards (2). Yet they left as a family.
Whereas the faith and courage of Abraham are asked of you:

' "Leave your native land and your ancestral home for the coun-
try which I shall show you." – Abram left, as Yahweh had told
him (3).'

It is not written that he hesitated or changed his mind. Throw
everything overboard, be quick about it. Accommodations and
delays will only increase the cost of the sacrifices to which one day

you will certainly have to consent, or never be a hermit or be able to persevere. God, summoning you to these renunciations, will be your strength. He brought the Jews out of Egypt 'in manu forti'.

> 'God does not untie, he tears;
> He does not bend, he breaks;
> He does not divide so much as breaks and ravages all.'

Thus Bossuet, speaking of the Virgin Mary (4).
    Later, you will understand this saying of God's:

'You have seen for yourselves how I carried you away on eagle's wings and brought you to myself (5).'

Do not try the weight of your cross; your heart may fail you. Put your trust in Him who out of love accepts you for what you are, regardless of your unworthiness, saying to himself:

> 'I am going to lure (him) away,
> lead (him) into the desert
> and speak to (his) heart (6).'

The desert is both fascinating and terrifying. It is the great, lonely void, and human beings instinctively dread being brought face to face with themselves. The Hermit is indeed a man apart. The essence of the desert is the absence of man; pure desert will not even tolerate life. The sea of sand, like the frozen mountain peaks, is nature in its virgin state as it issued from the Creator's hands; on it still seems to repose the Spirit of God which hovered over the waters at the beginning of the world (7). Rich souls are tempted by the virginity of the site. The desert is pure, and purifies. Where man is not, is neither sin nor rumour of the business of the world.

You will find the solitude good, but you will have to face its austerity. God himself defined the desert as:

'a land of steppe and ravine, a land of drought and danger, a land
through which no one passes and where no human being lives
(8).'
Immured in yourself, you will sometimes feel a yearning for human
conversation and the desert will seem horribly empty and mean-
ingless. You are not there as a tourist but are stuck there like a
nomad, without hope of return. In those 'desert combats' of which
St Benedict writes, you will have no support worth having except
God, even if he seems to become remote. It is written:

'The desert does not sustain the weakling,
it crushes him.
Who makes the effort and fights back can survive (9).'

This is true, and makes you think. You will have to learn to solve
your own problems, and your only safeguard will be a faith
finely-tempered. By humble prayer may you become one of those
athletes 'capable, by God's help, and with the sole vigour of their
own hand and arm, of doing battle with the vices of the flesh and
spirit 10.'
You used to love being alone, to relax, to draw breath in the
midst of activities keeping you interested in life and stimulating your
need to be productive. From now on, solitude will be your environ-
ment for a life-time and no one has any further interest in what you
produce. Now, there is only one thing you can do: pour out, apparently in pure loss, the precious perfume of your human qualities
at Jesus's feet. If you consent to this, you will be amply rewarded.
Defend the frontiers of your desert. What good would an
enclosure be to you if you allowed human beings to invade it by
newspapers, letters, visits? Do not forget that its very essence is
absence of people.
For you, the desert is not a setting, it is a state of soul. This is
where the difficulty lies. The centre of this solitude is you, in whom
the absence of human beings and human vanities creates a first zone
of silence. On the steppe there is only one sound: the moaning of the
wind. 'This is,' runs an Arabic proverb, 'the desert weeping because
it would like to be a meadow.' It is for you, O arid, waterless land,
to beg the Lord to distil his dew on you. Only the breathing of the

Spirit should be heard. Do not seek to people the silence with memories, with pictures of the past, with worldly speculations or distractions, left over from your life in society. The desert does not allow any compromise; it brutally obliges you to make a choice: between the inhospitable path, the endless advance with the bare minimum of baggage — or death. It neither offers nor admits any amusement. You would lose everything; the dilettante would kill the contemplative. The rustic monotony of the hermitage would soon grow wearisome to you, the lure of the world would torment you. You would languish like an uprooted plant, of cruel thirst. Twice unhappy, you would be deprived of the object of your desires and God would keep you at a distance. Oh yes, the desert is the land of thirst. As with Hagar, (11) as with Elisha on the way to Horeb, (12) you will come to think that death is upon you. Do not retrace your steps; God will sustain you.

The sequestered life is not easy; only by strict self-discipline will you succeed in establishing this second layer of silence.

Persevere, work at reducing your faculties to a unity, to the simplicity of silence. In the silence, it will not be long before you are visited by God. He came to Elisha on Horeb at a moment of such silence that the murmuring of the slightest breeze could be heard (13). When the Lord wants to raise a soul to contemplation, he obliges all its faculties to be silent, so as to commit itself to him alone. Stop bothering about yourself. When you no longer listen to nature's complaints, when you refuse to give a hearing to all anxiety, to all desire but that of love, when you become indifferent to your earthly lot, when you hardly think about yourself either for good or ill and no longer care about the approval of others; when, in a word, you have habitually lost sight of self, you will have penetrated the silent Holy of Holies, the inviolable sanctuary of your soul where God resides and whither he invites you. Of you, as of Moses, he will say:

'He is in charge of my whole household.
    I speak to him face to face,
plainly and not in riddles,
        and he sees Yahweh's glory (14).'

The whole spirituality of the desert is summed up in these deep words of St John of the Cross:

'The Father only utters one Word, that is to say, his Son, in an eternity of silence. He is saying it forever. The soul too must hear it in silence (15).'

Have you sometimes thought that the Word is being uttered in you? This sublime hearing is the whole eremitical life. You should be insatiable in listening to this Word, and no one but the Father – not books, not theologians – can make you hear it:

'No one can come to me
unless drawn by the Father who has sent me (16).'

This eternal word will be your food; scripture, eucharist, contemplation will dispense it to you. You will taste God's manna (17). The Holy Spirit will guide your soul towards it with infinitely more sweetness and suppleness that the luminous cloud (18). He will instruct you, as from an inner Sinai, in law of the Perfect Ones (19). With you, God will conclude his espousals (20) and in your heart will tell you how to please him with the liturgy of love for which he has reserved you (21). From the very heart of your aridity, he will cause the water of his grace to well up, to appease your thirst – gifts which will allow you to drink of the very life-source of the Trinity (22). In you will be renewed the 'magnalia Dei', provided that you courageously consent to tread the steppe.

For you have to keep on walking. The hermitage is not the Promised Land; it is not lawful for you to become ensconced there in the comfort of cherished habits or in self-centred tranquility. No, on your feet, with your gown hitched up and your staff in your hand is the way you have to eat this Passover. You are a pilgrim with no home, no baggage, no assurance for the morrow. The desert, for the man who ventures into it, is not a home but a track along which he hurries to reach, to use a lovely image, 'the bourne from which no traveller returns'. The bourne is God himself seen clear; and only death can show us that. Love must goad you on and make you incapable, as it were, of finding any pleasure in building a confortable shelter.

'Like a doe crying out for running water,
    my soul cries aloud for you, O God.
My soul is thirsty for God, O Living God!
    How soon shall I drink deep of God's presence (23)?'

He alone knows the moment and the way. Have no plan for your life, just keep yourself free of anything that could prevent God from moving you as he wishes. Tastes and distastes are not to be considered. Be available and malleable. The chosen people only knew one thing: that they were marching to the Promised Land, not knowing what intervening stages there would be. In that exodus, the Lord took the initiative all the time. They halted, they set out, they aligned their march on the cloud-signal alone and followed that blindly (24). The same abandonment is required of you, reposing in faith on the wisdom, the power and the love of your Heavenly Father.

'He knows all,
    he can do all
        and he loves me.'

Engrave this on your heart and on the palms of your hands. Moses chanted God's maternal solicitude, and the hermit must entrust himself to this. Moses is speaking of you when he says:

In the desert uplands he adopts him,
    in the horrible loneliness of the wilds.
He protects him, rears him, guards him
    like the pupil of his eye.
Like an eagle watching its nest,
    hovering over its young,
he spreads out his wings to hold him,
    he supports him on his pinions.
Yahweh alone is his guide.
    No alien god for him (25)!

You risk so much by hesitating to fling yourself into this abyss. If you want to 'make something of your life', God may perhaps agree, with these terrible words:

'I shall hide my face from (him)
and see what happens to (him) then (26).'

One can easily guess: you will perish of thirst and hunger in a kind of life which will not tolerate mediocrity, and you will be a 'worldling' under the hermit's smock.

2. John the Baptist's Wilderness

Under Christ's roof

' *"Rabbi, where do you live?"*
"Come and see (1)" '

No thought should be more familiar to you than that your vocation is a free gift from God and that it is eternal, with all its host of favours.

'You did not choose me,
   no, I chose you (2).'

'Before I formed you in the womb,
   I knew you (3).'

'Yahweh called me from my mother's womb:
   he pronounced my name (4).'

This is as true of you as of Jeremiah, of Isaiah, of Israel, of John the Baptist, of Paul. Your call to the desert is as eternal as everything else concerning you, and it has its source in God's inexplicable predilection for you. You will sing the singular mercy of the

Lord for all eternity. Whatever the circumstances or conscious personal motives determining your resolution – as for Jesus – the Holy Spirit it is who has led you into the desert (5). As with the Forerunner, God has hidden you in his hand (6), that fatherly hand which has fashioned you and which erects round you a protective rampart and dispenses to you his grace, enfolding you in his tender embrace. It separates you from the profane and consecrates you exclusively to the service of his love. It preserves you from the untoward approach of creatures, it defends you against your own proclivity to reach your arms out to them. Its contact quickens you, purifies you, warms you. By him alone you live and to him you owe all your natural and supernatural resources. The Hermit's desert is not a nightmare gaol in which he is forcibly shut away. Have faith enough to realise that, being there, you are 'a nursling carried at the breast and fondled in the lap. Like a son being comforted by his mother,' God will comfort you (7). Then 'your heart will rejoice and your bones will flourish like the grass (8).'

Like the Forerunner, you were intended for Christ, not merely in the sense in which St Paul means that all the elect have been foreordained (9), but because the only reason for your existence on earth is to love and glorify Jesus. You are more than the Bridegroom's friend. Your soul is truly the Bride, and you will make the outpourings of the mystic marriage-song your own: 'I am my Beloved's and my Beloved is mine (10).'

St John the Baptist did not live on intimate terms with Christ; you are luckier than he, for you have the eucharist and know all the marvels of grace.

You have the right to hope to receive 'the kiss of his mouth' promised to those who leave all to follow him, and the desert will become 'a garden of spices' where the Beloved 'pastures his flock among the lilies (11).' In this sense, 'the least in the kingdom of heaven is greater than he is (12).'

Take care to keep your hermitage austere. Since contemplation is the highest exercise of charity, you will sometimes be rudely tempted to lay aside that harshness of life exemplified by all anchorites. John the Baptist who was one of the purest of the pure allowed his body only the barest necessities to keep alive. The world needs atonement, and you are not without sin, nor without perverse inclinations. If the Forerunner had witnessed the Passion, he would have been athirst to follow the Bridegroom to martyrdom. He was granted the grace to shed his blood, but perhaps without the light of the Cross in which you bathe. Be happy if the hermitage offers you the maximum of discomfort – so detestable to modern taste. Time-saving, higher productivity, freedom of mind are often no more than alibis. The hermit has no cause whatever to gear the rhythm of his life to the frenetic course of a world whose scale of values is the reverse of his. He feeds on eternity.

In the temporal domain he has no desires, he only has needs; let him beware of creating others for himself. Let inconvenience in all things be familiar to you; 'no-need' should order your arrangements and requirements. Better for you if obedience acts as a brake, not as a goad. The natural desert bristles against all sensuality and this is why there are few lovers in it. But those whom it seduces have experienced that from the harshly treated body the spirit emerges in purity and light. Without this taste for austerities, how can you become a successor to the martyrs?

May you be worthy of the eulogy pronounced by Jesus over the Baptist: 'John was a lamp alight and shining (13)' (lucerna ardens et lucens). Because the hermit burns, burns himself up, he gives light like the sanctuary lamp.

He burns himself up by purity, which stifles the appetites of the flesh. He burns himself by penance, which causes him to renounce the sources of earthly joy. Above all, he burns himself up by love, which is a fire. The heat of this flame kindled by the Holy Spirit wore out the very bodies of the mystics and delivered the Virgin Mary's soul from its earthly bonds. Jesus Christ must be your passion, and the zeal for his glory in you and in others. Perhaps you will be given the grace of longing for his coming and of making the Bride's lament in Revelation your own: 'Come!' Then it will be said to you: 'Let all who are thirsty come! All who want the water of life can have it free (14)!' The emptiness, the aridity, the austerity of the desert urge your steps along the path which leads to the land of rest. Instantly John forgot the weariness of those harsh years of preparation when he saw the Lamb of God standing before him, whose ways he had been making plain (15). Then he had only one wish: 'He must grow greater and I must grow smaller (16),' not

only in renown but as spiritual entity, foreseeing that sublime ideal
formulated by St Paul:

> 'I live now not with my own life
> but with the life of Christ who lives in me (17).'

And thus the little lamp burns out by becoming divine.

For you, the Messiah's coming is not in the future. You live under Jesus's roof. You feed day by day on his flesh, his life gives you
life, his Spirit guides and urges you on, you are dead and risen again
with Him. Why should your charity merely smoulder under the
ash? The eremitical life can only be explained by the need to share a
great love. It must be so. In the Mystical Body of Christ, your job
is to be the heart; if not, what are you, you who have neither works
nor preaching, and do not even administer the sacraments?

Your hidden life speaks to the world, but only gives light in so
far as it fuses with concentrated love. The Forerunner was a peerless
witness to Jesus Christ, being charged with the mission to point him
out: 'Here he is', 'Ecce'. You too, in Church and world, are his
witness, but what speaks in you is not the tongue, but your state,
your very self. Your life is true to the teaching, to the example of
Jesus Christ, and the ardour of your faith seen in your actions brings
others to reflect on the transcendence of the One who inspires that
ardour:

> 'Your light must shine in the sight of men, so that, seeing your
> good works, they may give praise to your Father in heaven (18).'

The perfect image of the Son, which you are predestined to become,
turns people's minds to the Exemplar (19). You fulfil that saying of
St Paul's:

> 'In our body we always carry Jesus's death, so that in our body
> Jesus's life may also be seen (20).'

Jesus is God. Since this is so, you are a witness to God, whom
you reflect as in a mirror (21). By having renounced creatures, you
proclaim their nothingness before God's Majesty. By having
renounced the joys which they afford, you proclaim the sufficiency

of God, who is our Supreme Bliss. By your exclusive application to prayer, you proclaim his infinite Majesty and Sovereignty. And your witness has all the more force, the more hidden and silent is your life, lived in contemplation of God's supreme transcendence.

It radiates far further than human beings can imagine. It is not enough that the testimony be given: it has to be received. This is not a matter of presentation but a matter of grace. God alone opens men's eyes to its light. Be it as dazzling as it may, a blind man will not see it. The Word, having come into this world, 'was the light of men, a light that shone in the dark, a light that darkness could not overpower (22)'. By your prayer and sacrifices, you will win the grace for others to be docile to the testimony. Jesus preached a great deal, but he attributed the fruits of his apostolate to the mute offering on Calvary:

'When I am lifted from the earth,
    I shall draw all men to myself (23).'

You are a true forerunner, smoothing the path. But you will need the faith that moves mountains, if you are to believe that your prayer is efficacious in so humble and denuded a way of life.

John believed in his mission; believe in yours. He did not seek his own advancement; he did nothing to leave his solitude and slip into Jesus's privileged company. Friend of the Bridegroom, he rejoiced in the Bridegroom's joy, happy himself to endure the terrible loneliness of the dungeons of Machaerus, which he was never to leave until face to face with God forever. That Jesus did not call him to join the Apostolic College, to the founding of the Church, to the bliss of intimacy with him, did not signify a love any the less tender. None of the Apostles was to receive higher praise from Jesus than the man whom he held to be 'much more than a prophet (24)'. 'I tell you solemnly, of all the children born of women, a greater than John the Baptist has never been seen (25)'. His it was to be the encouraging model for souls prepared to renounce everything, the sweetness of God's consolations included, so that in them and by them the God of all consolation might be glorified. It is no light thing to be so utterly forgetful of self and to endure the supreme austerity of God's silence in the desert without losing either faith or hope.

The Forerunner understood Jesus's mysterious attitude to him and, in the calm liveliness of his faith, 'through Christ' though far away, 'his consolation overflowed (26)'. His was the happiness of aged Simeon: of seeing all the scriptures being fulfilled in him and of contemplating the dawning of the world's salvation (27). Having received no other ministry in the new economy, he offered himself in the silence of contemplation. Indeed, as friend of the Bridegroom, he too was the Bride, and from the Visitation onward had never left the bridal chamber, where the Word filled him with light . . .

———————————

Let the light on your dark path be this maxim of St John of the Cross:

'Love does not consist in feeling great things but in knowing great deprivation and great suffering for the Beloved (28).'

3. Jesus's Wilderness

Combat in the desert

'The spirit drove him into the wilderness . . .
He remained in the wilderness . . .
*   tempted by Satan (1).'*

St Mark relates that no sooner had Jesus come out of the water after his baptism, than 'he saw the heavens torn apart and the Spirit like a dove, descending on him (2)'. And when the Father's voice rang out, 'immediately afterwards,' the Evangelist goes on, 'the Spirit drove him into the wilderness (3)'. Note the connection which the text seems to establish betweeen the fulness of the Spirit resting on Jesus and his withdrawal into the wilderness. This is a mystery which affects the Hermit more nearly than anyone.

The word pronounced by the Father was a word of love: 'You are my beloved Son; my favour rests on you (4).' The Spirit given was the Spirit of Love. Christ's withdrawal into the wilderness was a loving response to this word, this gift of love. The Son of God had no need to prepare for the apostolate. But his human nature, most particularly at this overwhelming moment, aspired to be alone with his Father. Guardini was right in thinking that the Spirit, 'forced him out into the wilds, far from his dear ones, far from the people on the banks of Jordan, somewhere where there was no one but his Father and him (5)'.

You may not have experienced the action of grace leading you to the hermitage quite as clearly as this. Sometimes a set of quite profane circumstances seem to be responsible, seem to push you, rather than your being in command of them. Not you, but someone else, the Holy Spirit, is in control, making all these factors cohere to bring you here. He it is who has 'forced you out into the wilds'. You can only give one possible response: loving acquiescence; perseverance in the desert permits no other. Pope Pius XII said this clearly:

'Not fear, not penance, not prudence alone peoples the solitude of our monasteries, but love of God (6).'

It will not take you long to fix ungenerous limits to your acts of atonement; the spirit of the age sets its face against protracted mourning. Insatiable for love, it exults in its own abilities. Yours however is the right to free your mind and heart from the contingencies of worldly life, to apply all their resources to eternal truths, to Truth Supreme, God who is 'light' (7) and 'love' (8).

Do not expect however to be at rest forthwith. Jesus, despite his purity and holiness, imposed a superhuman fast on himself, symbolically portraying the struggle which you will have to wage to establish the calm supremacy of all the virtues in you. He confronted the Devil face to face and overthrew him, to warn you of the battles which await you, and to teach you how to be victorious. You will build the ramparts of your soul with your trowel in one hand and your sword in the other (9). It is longer, harder work pacifying your soul than you may think. Between the 'sincerity' of your efforts and the 'truth' of your renunciations is a great gulf; it will not be long before you learn this to be so.

You are going into the desert, not with Jesus's innocence, but with the essential corruptness of your nature, made worse by the distortions and wounds inflicted on it by your habits and sins. You have broken your links with the world, not by tearing up pieces of paper, but by slashing into living matter, and the vigorous stumps of your affections have not yet stopped sprouting. You will often be tempted to feel sorry for yourself. Inflexible fidelity to obedience will save you.

The Rule under which you fight will be your great purifier and pacifier, even if it seems as remorseless as a rolling-mill. It will impose an absolute fast on your self-esteem, whatever form that may take, and will gradually re-establish the hierarchy and harmony of all natural and supernatural virtues in you. Order assures peace of mind: this is what St Augustine called 'peace'. The hermitage promises you this, while warning you that it is an armed peace, and that lack of vigilance, energy or prayer can put everything in jeopardy. Our peace is precarious because within us we bear both the foes that threaten it and the accomplices betraying our defences. Yet it is already something, to have put a distance between your passions and their objects. Take heart: 'Our actions alter us,' writes Fr de Montcheuil (10). The renunciations which seem to cost so much today will, if you make them generous-heartedly, lose their initial bitterness. Charity as it grows will one day make you love what seems repugnant now, while dry and needy faith is still more powerful than love forgetful of self-satisfaction.

The devil is no myth, and if it is going too far to see him in your every temptation, the entire monastic tradition agrees in ascribing a particular fury against anchorites to him. The desert was reputed, as witness the Gospel (11), to be the very place which he inhabited; and the monk, taking a hazardous offensive, did his best to dislodge him. St Matthew makes an explicit connection between Jesus's withdrawal into the wilderness, and temptation:

'Jesus was led by the Spirit into the wilderness,
to be tempted by the Devil there (12).'

Awareness of your habitual weaknesses, past experience and the particular painfulness of certain sacrifices should all alert you to the struggles which are to come. The desert offers a number of classic struggles, which you will be hard put to it to win: the desert's own excellent qualities provoke them. It is often bewilderingly hard to fight these insubstantial, hence invulnerable, inner monsters.

Solitude shelters you from the world's attempts to pervert you. Not seeing, not hearing, not smelling, not touching sets you deep in a zone of relative safety. But a danger awaits you: that turning in on yourself which gives rise to an eccentric sensibility, a sort of undue

exacerbation of the emotions and imagination, by which dispropor-
tionate importance is attached to the most trivial things, thus
threatening you with the perils of obsession. Inner ordeals blow up,
the puerile objects of which trouble your peace and cause much suffering. Were you leading the active life, you would shrug your
shoulders and that would be that. In the desert, these phantoms
keep harassing you. God can use this susceptibility to suffering as a
means of purging your soul. But the devil with his wiles can profit
from it too. Opening your heart to an enlightened guide will save
you from a danger to which some people, alas, succumb: obsession,
persecution mania, scrupulosity, various forms of melancholia. The
ever-discontented and the blasé are the inept victims of the sequestered life. The mystics are its most successful products . . .

The fast imposed by the desert on your faculties — the ordinary
satisfactions of which normally safeguard human well-being and
happiness — will make the primacy of the spirit triumphant in you.
Your instincts however are indestructible and you will never be able
to stop your heart and flesh from being moved. God was the
architect of the structure: you must neither deplore nor try to wreck
this admirable arrangement. Mastering these instincts is a delicate
business.

Memory and imagination will go on provoking impatience with
privation, and the devil has direct access to our senses. Not uncom-
monly, those most pure are prey to the least avowable temptations
or to the most desperate emotional attachments.

You must humbly accept, pray, preserve peace and trust.
Resisting these impulses is a fine act of faith, hope and love; it is also
one of the austerest forms of penance. Believe that this is the purifying crucible, into which scores of holy souls have been thrown: the
lives of the Desert Fathers will reassure you. The devil will lose a
match if, instead of panicking, you calmly agree that you are only
human, not an angel, and that you are going to God on foot and not
on seraph's wings.

Contemplation too, that most godlike act, that most perfect exercise of charity, can engender the subtlest temptations, at least at its
first stage when it involves more acquisition than infusion. Pride has
no power over the genuine mystic: the intense activity of the gift of
fear reduces him to powder. You cannot be a mystic for the asking.

He who has succeeded, to quote St Benedict, having subdued the vices of flesh and spirit, 'by the lawful delight in the other-worldly realities for which he has forsaken all, in tasting how sweet the Lord is (14), may stumble into the snare of vain complacency and presumption. To him, the devil will suggest that he belongs to the 'aristocracy' of the spiritual world and persuade him that, having passed the stage of apprenticeship, he can plunge uncontrolledly into the way of exceptional penances or, contrariwise, relax his rigour and let the reins go slack: 'If you are the Son of God, throw yourself down (15)!' Humility's reply is easy: I cannot throw myself down, because I am not up. I should have to advance a great deal further in perfection for it to make any appreciable difference. What can I do but go on trusting and obeying?

Obeying your guide, but obeying the Holy Spirit, the Spirit of Jesus, who has led you into the desert. If you are genuinely a man of prayer, you are safe. What did Jesus do in solitude, not preaching, not eating, not drinking, possibly not sleeping? He contemplated. His whole soul was before God, all his powers deployed in contemplation, freed from every other sort of activity. The beatific light bathed his mind; his will burned with heavenly charity. The gifts of the Holy Spirit bore all their fruits in him. Disengaged from all earthly occupations, Jesus could give his prayer a scope never to be exceeded again during his ministry.

Yours will be more modest and intermittent. But at least let the desire to be with God goad you as often and as intensely as it may. Tirelessly plead with him to give himself to you. Mystical prayer is part of your vocation as Christian and hermit. Ask for this favour, in peaceful humility accepting that it may be deferred or refused. Do your best to make yourself ready for the gift when God eventually bestows it.

You will do nothing but contemplate forever. The monk's vocation is eschatological: he tries to live by anticipation as the blessed ones live. Shut off from the side facing earth, the desert's only view is towards heaven. And the trail which you are following has no end, except in God. Be generous: not angels will draw near to serve you, but the Master himself, who will put on his apron, seat you at table and serve you (16).

4. Mary Magdalen's Wilderness

Compunction

'Her many sins must have been forgiven her,
or she would not have shown so much love (1).'

Let us accept the tradition by which Mary Magdalen is venerated in the wilderness of Sainte-Baume in Provence. For this is the guise in which she is honoured as a patroness of monasticism. Meditate on the passages about her in the Gospel and follow her in heart to her retreat. She will be of great comfort to you. You are not better than she, you no more deserve the Lord's mercy than she did. Indeed, in her transgressions, she had ignorance for an excuse, which you cannot have. What you do have in common is both being lost sheep whom the Saviour has followed and brought back to the sheepfold on his shoulder (2).

What did she do in the wilderness? She atoned, no doubt, by harsh penances. Above all, she remembered with piercing clarity that unforgettable look which Jesus had turned on her. Do you sometimes think about Christ's extraordinary gaze, the beneficent power of which is often mentioned in the Gospel? 'He looked at her, and he loved her.'

For you, as for the Magdalen, the phrase must be inverted: he loves you and has looked at you. He loved you first (3). In the desert, you should live under this gaze. God never takes his eyes off you. It is good not to forget that 'his eyes are forever watching, assaying human beings one by one (4)' and that 'the eyes of Yahweh are everywhere, observing the wicked and the good' (5) and that all your deeds are 'in his ledger (6).'

Do not think of his gaze as being glacial and terrifying. Even in justice, God is still a Father. Even when you were hardly concerned about him at all and were drinking sin like water, he was lowering his merciful gaze on you: his grace was penetrating you to lead you to repentance. He lets others die in their sin. Why this preference for you? 'I have loved Jacob, I have hated Esau.' Why? St Paul replies: 'He has mercy on whom he pleases, and he hardens whom he pleases.' He is not accountable to us. 'O man, who are you to argue with God (7)?'

Ceaselessly the Magdalen ruminated over the incomprehensible mercy, the fascinating tenderness, which she had first glimpsed in Jesus's eye in the house of Simon the Pharisee. She had thought to take the initiative by her expensive gesture, but the grace of Christ was in fact attracting her. He saw her from afar in her perplexity, as he saw Nathanael under the figtree (8), and invisibly dictated what actions her soul should perform by giving her the energy to perform them. His will it was that bent the sinner's knee and clove her heart. And so it was with you. Magdalen could then raise her eyes to his, revealing a soul now purified, transfigured and afire. Never was she to forget Christ's look as he said:

'Your sins are forgiven . . .
Your faith has saved you; go in peace (9)',

anymore than she would that look of heavenly bliss which he directed on her as she sat at his feet contemplating the Word made flesh in him (10), or that look of noble gratitude acknowledging the anointing at Bethany. The eyes of Jesus were the light of her cavern in Provence.

Poignant awareness of her past disorders constantly revived new amazement at the privileges of which she felt unworthy but which she nonetheless accepted unreservedly, with rapt heart — so lively was her faith in God's forgiveness.

You cannot be happy in the desert unless you share this very faith. Men do not know how to forgive. Perhaps you will always find Simons to reproach you with your faults, as though very often they supposed their own virtuousness was not a matter of chance. Sinful man remembers; offended God forgets.

'Though your sins are like scarlet,
    they shall be as white as snow;
though they are as red as crimson,
    they shall be like wool (11).'

He has cast 'behind his back' all our sins, and they will not come back to life in his memory (12). Take these avowals of God's to heart:

'Is Ephraim my dearest son,
    is he my favourite child,
that whenever I mention him
    I still think of him with longing?
Deeply yearning for him,
    I must have pity on him (13).'

Compunction is not genuine without this trustful, calming certitude. To be mistrustful of having been forgiven is an insult to God's fatherly heart. If the hermit weeps at the memory of his transgressions, let them be tears of joy. God restores more wonderfully than he creates. If nothing is final in the spiritual life, so nothing is irreparable either. 'No,' wrote Fr de Foucauld, 'my past sins did not frighten me ... Men do not forgive, because they cannot give back purity once lost; God forgives, because he wipes out the very stains and fully restores the original beauty (14).'

The devil can, of course, discourage you. But why should his lies carry more weight than the word of God? —

'I have formed you, you are my servant ... I have dispelled your rebellion like a cloud and your sins like a mist. Come back to me, for I am your avenger (15).'

'By my own self I swear it; what comes from my mouth is true, a word irrevocable (16).'

Even so, you are determined to atone? You will do this better by the fire of love than by ferocious maceration. Do you think that Magdalen won her pardon cheaply? Love only asked one thing of her: to climb up Calvary, to stand at the foot of the Cross and contemplate the appalling torment of that most sublime object of her love. She would not be allowed to say one word or make one gesture to soften his sufferings or to encourage him. Thus the sinful woman made satisfaction there in the most astounding and terrible of ways.

And there she learned what she had not known before: the horror and spite of the offence offered to the majesty of the Transcendant God. Her sin, in the perspective of the smiling Christ of Bethany, had human proportions. On Calvary, she suddenly becomes aware of the immensity of her fault, when the rigour of the Father's justice is revealed, not even sparing his only Son (17). She must see for herself what infinitely costly reparation is exacted for an infinitely wicked offence: her own. Anticipating St Paul, she could say: 'He loved me and sacrificed himself for my sake' (18). Try to feel the distractedness, the brokenness of her devoted heart. In her visual memory she keeps those last glances of Jesus: charged with sadness, anguish, fear and strange flashes of what seemed like despair: 'My God, my God, why have you deserted me?' (19)

The Magdalen was spared nothing: blasphemies, cries of hatred, jokes, the sound of the hammers, the groans of the sufferer rack her nerves and her heart. And at the very centre of the scene, she contemplates the torment of the Saviour's every muscle, whose body is but one vast wound, and sees the horrible effects of his falls. Now she discovers what pride, sensuality, unlawful loves and selfishness cost God. Her sin is stripped of the concrete circumstances which gave it its bewitching charm. When Jesus cries out for thirst, the Magdalen, no more than the Virgin Mary, was authorised to proffer help.

What a crucible those dramatic hours were for this lover of Christ! What a punishment for her sins, what frightful satisfaction was exacted! For her, the wine-press of the Cross had to squeeze her heart of its wicked pleasures to the last drop.

Her only consolation was to be looked at for one last time by Jesus as he turned his head towards his Mother to say: 'Woman, this is your son' (20). But what an expression in those eyes, drowned in tears, sweat, blood and already veiled by the shadow of death! Magdalen wondered how they could be the same ones as gazed at her in Bethany . . .

Such was Mary Magdalen's share in Christ's Passion, the final act of divine forgiveness, a more onerous satisfaction, though only lasting for a moment, than a lifetime of fasting, vigils and self-discipline. Probably in her inner wilderness, no day went by without her reliving those climactic hours of human history, which had been her Calvary too . . .

In your hermitage, love to meditate on Jesus's passion in the way that it concerns you, as the Magdalen, as St Paul and as hosts of other saints have done. Pascal puts a saying too restricted into Christ's mouth: 'I shed such and such a drop of blood for you.' No, all the Precious Blood at once was shed for each of us. Perhaps you will want to sing each of the Canonical Hours in union with Christ at such and such a moment of his martyrdom, to spend a little while each day on Calvary, if only by explicitly evoking the Saviour's bloody sacrifice by hearing Mass.

You complain of stony-heartedness at the memory of your faults. Perhaps the metaphysics of repentance have not made much impression on you yet. If you attain to passionately loving Jesus, none of his torments will leave you unmoved, and the conviction that you have been in part responsible for them will plunge the goad of regret and detestation into your heart. Do not concentrate too much on analysing your feelings. True contrition cannot abolish a certain natural animal enjoyment, a certain subtle charm, in the memory of the pleasure enjoyed. Be sorry for the offence offered to God, even if you cannot manage to feel detestation for the pleasure which seduced you. The Lord sees more clearly into the depths of your soul then you can; leave the judging to him. Happy Peter, whose tears of contrition dug trenches down his cheeks! This is of grace. It takes time to go down so deep into one's wretchedness; you only learn the wickedness of your sin by process of atoning for it.

The hermit's heart must break or soften at God's approach: if not, how can it open to the call of the Beloved desiring you to share your table with him? —

'Look, I am standing at the door, knocking;
    if one of you hears me calling and opens the door,
I shall come in to share his meal,
    side by side with him (21).'

You must be pure. Strive to achieve that delicacy of conscience
which is not scruple but a sense of sin. This is the fruit of the spirit of
adoration and of the gift of fear. Daily confession is the most en-
couraged in eremitical orders.

Compunction is always shot through with reflections of the glory
of the resurrected Christ — otherwise it becomes black despair. The
Magdalen knew this better than anyone, she having been the first to
see the Lord on Easter morning. Forgetting nothing of the horrors
of Golgotha, in her wilderness she went on hearing the unique ring
of Jesus's voice, calling her by her familiar name: 'Mary!' For at
that moment she had seen the Bethany gaze radiant with a glorious
majesty assuring her of her future bliss. From that day, Mary
Magdalen lived the resurrectional life, as was to be defined by St
Paul. Following her example, monks have fixed their sights beyond
this world, striving to live as though they had already passed
through the Gates of Eternity.

'For us,' writes the Apostle, 'our homeland is in heaven, and from
heaven comes the Saviour we so earnestly await, the Lord Jesus
Christ, and he will transfigure these wretched bodies of ours into
copies of his glorious body. He will do that by the same power with
which he can subdue the whole universe (22)'.

Awareness of sin must send the soul leaping towards those
heights. The history of our personal fall must not stop short at the
avowal of it, be that never so humble. It is followed by its redemption and ends in glory. The saying in the Epistle to the Philippians
is an invitation to holiness repeated by St Paul on numerous oc-
casions, based on the fact of Jesus's corporeal resurrection as confirmation of our own spiritual resurrection. The Magdalen had indeed
died to sin, and her heart was where her treasure was: Jesus Christ,
triumphant in heaven.

The hermit sees his destiny of grace lighting up his solitude. But
only on condition that until his latest breath he has the will-power to
ask nothing of the earth, taking the Apostle's instruction literally:

'Since you have been brought back to true life with Christ, you must look for the things that are in heaven, where Christ is, sitting at God's right hand. Let your thoughts be on heavenly things, not on the things that are on the earth, because you have died, and now the life you have is hidden with Christ in God. But when Christ is revealed — and he is your life — you too will be revealed in all your glory with him (23).'

Since God has showered such privileges on you, try to be the joy of his heart. In the wilderness of this world, try to be a succulent fruit of his grace.

'Like finding grapes in the wilderness,
  I found Israel (24).'

5. St Paul's Wilderness

Discovering Christ

'For me, life is Christ (1).'

We rarely speak of St Paul's withdrawal into the desert immediately after his conversion. He only tells us of it incidentally:

'Then God, who had specially chosen me while I was still in my mother's womb, called me through his grace and chose to reveal his Son to me, so that I might preach the Good News about him to the pagans. I did not stop to discuss this with any human being, nor did I go up to Jerusalem to see those who were already apostles before me, but I went off at once to Arabia (2).'

The expression 'not discussing this with any human being' — literally 'without consulting flesh and blood' — allows us to imagine the horror of his decision: the links to be broken, the unknown to be faced. Paul did not argue: he acted, as he had done on the road to Damascus. In God's hands, he was vowed to service, to slavery even (3), and the prospect of a sacrifice, even the sacrifice of life itself, never deterred or delayed him in his obedience. He too, like Jesus, was thrown out by the Holy Spirit and driven into the wilds.

Have you more to break with than the Apostle had? You are not being asked to renounce your religion, your people, your friendships, to join a sect which you have hitherto been persecuting, for the best of motives be it said. But each man has his own well-loved 'Isaac' to sacrifice. . . Do not hesitate. You are entering a desert rich in the spiritual treasure which Paul found and brought out of it. His life was more upset than yours will be. Custom dulls the pangs of Christian life. Why is Jesus Christ, your soul's friend since baptism, of so little account to you? Beg God to lead you on a road to Damascus where a meeting with Jesus can throw you to the ground and make you his prisoner forever, a prisoner of love and hence a prisoner of the desert (4).

Receiving such a resounding shock from Christ does not depend on you. A single sentence chained the Apostle irrevocably: 'I am Jesus, and you are persecuting me' (5). Paul fled into the desert with this revelation. He needed to be alone to study it, to extract all the light and love from it. He was to yield up all his vitality to this first touch.

'By God's grace I am what I am, and the grace which he gave me has not been fruitless (6).'

With the impetuosity of youth and the violence of his temperament, the fire of charity enflaming him, Paul would have made a fearsome anchorite. He was cut out to be one, but his vocation lay elsewhere. The austerities of his apostolate were by far to exceed the macerations of the desert (7).

However stern your way of life may be, you will never have to endure the Apostle's protracted suffering for Christ's sake (8).

In what respect, in his mysterious desert, can St Paul be your model? In this: that he shut himself away there with Jesus. Jesus light, Jesus charity. This should be all your contemplation, all your occupation. Because St Paul was destined for vast undertakings, God made that revelation an active and urgent one. But you: you have a lifetime to assess the measureless dimensions of the person, mission and teachings of the Incarnate Word. Bible in hand – for the hermit, the book of books – you are in possession of everything that God has said to men since the beginning of the world. The writers, the prophets, the Apostles, the Evangelists, St Paul himself, offer you the light by which they were themselves enlightened and which forever illuminates the Church. The Word of God became

'scripture' before becoming 'flesh' and 'bread'. Under these three
forms, he is your 'manna'. How then can you starve to death?

The centre, the summit, of this whole Revelation is Jesus Christ.
Paul withdrew into the wilds to ponder and savour God's extraordinary design for us, 'this mystery hidden for generations and centuries' which had just been revealed to him: 'Christ living with us
pagans (9).' Before the marvelling eyes of his soul, during those two
or three years as an anchorite, unfolded the prodigious history of
God's love for his creatures, throughout the length of which he saw
that Christ blaze forth who had just ravished his heart away (10).

This should be the habitual theme of your reflections: God's eternal design fulfilled in you during your earthly existence. The hermit
has no other ambition than to lend his hand to this in all good will.

Happy you, if the light wells up from your heart! Jesus was pleased first to show himself to Saul in the splendour of his glorified
flesh, no doubt with the moving details of the scars of his passion, to
give him a more vivid understanding of the simple words: 'Why are
you persecuting ME (11)?' Thenceforth, Paul loved the Saviour
with an almost savage love:

'The love of Christ overwhelms us . . . (12).'
'If anyone does not love the Lord, a curse on him (13)!'
'Nothing can come between us and the love of Christ (14).'

Spend many hours poring over the Gospel, so that Christ's person
may take life and depth for you. His human nature must become
familiar to you and his charm move you, as he captivated those who
had the good fortune to know him. In the mysteries of his earthly
life, the divine perfections which we are bound to imitate were
translated into terms which we can understand. Without him, this
command would have us at a loss:

'You must be perfect,
    just as your heavenly Father is perfect (15).'

In the desert, Paul realised that this perfection is revealed to us in
Jesus Christ — he, the faithful 'image of the unseen God' (16). Then,
in those enigmatic words uttered on the Damascus road, he dis-

covered the dazzling marvel of our unity with Christ, prefacing the
revelation of God's plan for man, which came to him soon
afterwards: God only accepts us in his Only Son in so far as we
belong to him or are like him:

'Before the world was made, he chose us, chose us in Christ, to be
holy and spotless, and to live through love in his presence, determining that we should become his adopted sons through Jesus
Christ (17).'

Progressively he identified those links intimately attaching us to the
Incarnate Word, Head of the Mystical Body, of which Paul and
we have become members (18), by baptism (19), quickened by his
Spirit, living by his life, and so able and obliged in a certain sense to
identify ourselves with him:

'I live now not with my own life
    but with the life of Christ who lives in me (20).'

It then seemed to him as though he had passed into another
world, the world to come, and that, dead to sin and risen with
Christ, he ought to live that eschatological life which was to inspire
the first Christians and generations of ascetics after them:

'For us, our homeland is in heaven (21).'
'You are fellow-citizens with the saints (22).'

'From the moment you are brought back to life with Christ, you
must look for the things that are in heaven, where Christ is ... For
you have died, and now the life you have is hidden with Christ in
God (23).'

His sole aspiration was to model himself on Christ. The Holy
Spirit drew his attention especially to the mystery of the Cross,
which had won him – as us – the right to pursue this vocation (24).
    His programme was the same as the hermit's is:

'The life I now live in this body I live in faith: faith in the Son of
God who loved me and who sacrificed himself for my sake (25).'

No one ever had a deeper understanding of the meaning of the Cross. By its light, the ex-Pharisee, so versed in knowledge of the scriptures, realised that he had not hitherto had the key to them, and found a new meaning in them, the only true one. He re-read the Bible and new light came flooding in. He deciphered the Pentateuch in the light of Jesus's priesthood; then, coming to himself, at the memory of his own sins and of his engrafting into Christ, burned to bear 'the marks of Jesus in his own body (26)', to 'treat his body hard' and 'reduce it to slavery (27)', and to pride himself on having been 'crucified with Christ (28)' and on having no other wisdom than that (29). Detached to the last fibre of his being from everything which was not divine and which he regarded as rubbish ('ut stercora') (30), executioner of his flesh, against which he battled 'not beating the air (31)', passionate student of the scriptures (32), raised to the highest peaks of contemplation (33), yearning to go and join Christ (34), St Paul had the stature of the greatest of ascetics.

Perhaps the desert would have kept him, had God not explicitly called him to the apostolate by granting him 'by a revelation, knowledge of the mystery of salvation through Christ (35)' and by entrusting him with the mission to proclaim it (36). The Holy Spirit infused him with overflowing love for the souls that were to compose the Mystical Body of Christ. He left his solitude with this unbridled ambition: 'to bring everything together under Christ, as head (37)', summed up in this device: 'He must be king (38).'

Called to the hermitage to live and die there, you have no need to travel the world, even in imagination, to spread the Good News. Do as the Apostle did in the desert. He is more than a model for you; he is your guide and spiritual father. Read his epistles over and over. They will help you to make an inventory of 'the infinite riches of the grace (of God) through his goodness towards us in Christ' (39), for Paul it was who was entrusted with 'proclaiming the infinite treasure of Christ and of explaining how it was to be dispensed (40).'

But what you lack, I suppose, is ardour in loving Jesus Christ. Admit the weakness of your devotion. All the same, your only chance of persevering in the desert — offering you no human interest and bristling with extenuating difficulties for you: your only chance is to cling to Jesus Christ. 'These are the trials,' the Apostle tells you, 'through which we triumph, by the power of Him who loves us' (41). There is nothing lovable about the desert as such; all too soon its tedium demoralises us. Its great spiritual value is to undo those bonds twined round our heart, and to drive our desires beyond it and higher: to God. By new bonds, it chains us to Christ, the sole companion on our journey.

The hermitage is not a stable dwelling. We camp in it under the world's canvass, to work a fundamental change as quickly and as thoroughly as we can: of stripping off the old man and putting on the new (42), that is to say, Jesus (43).

If you go into the wilds with other hopes, you will mistake your way and soon discover so. Saul offered himself to the Lord as a fresh page, as a new instrument. His life did not take the course which he thought it would. But he regretted nothing, even so.

Like him and for the same reason, nothing should alarm you.

'I know who it is that I have put my trust in, and I have no doubt at all that he is able to take care of all that I have entrusted to him until that day,' – the day I die (44).

What does it matter if you are weak? Who can boast of being strong in the battles of the Lord, if not he who leans with all his weight on Jesus Christ?

'There is nothing I cannot master with the help of Him who gives me strength (45).'

At your last hour, may you sincerely and truthfully be able to adopt as yours St Paul's judgment on his own life:

'I have fought the good fight to the end;
I have run the race to the finish;
I have kept the faith.

All there is to come now is the crown of righteousness reserved for me, which the Lord, the righteous Judge, will give me on that day: and not only to me but to all those who have longed for his appearing (46).'

6. The Desert of the Night

The crucible of the desert

'*Even the darkness is not very dark for you,
since for you the night shines like day (1).*'

For the hermit, night is the time of greatest proximity to God.
Night sweeps across the desert, making things insubstantial; they
lose their colours and contours to dissolve into a uniform sheet of
bluish shadow where nothing is discerned. The rhythm of time
seems to be suspended, stillness replaces succession, making one
aware of the nearness of eternity. Earth sleeps; all is silent. The sky
attracts the watcher's eyes towards 'the stars shining joyfully at their
posts . . . They shine to delight their Creator (2).'

The solitary on the threshold of his cell, waiting to answer the
bell for matins, hears the psalmist's words:

'The heavens proclaim God's glory,
   the sky displays his creative skill (3).'

God seems to be surrounding him everywhere, as though the hermit
were resting on God's bosom. Well with the young American pilot
may he say: 'I have reached out my hand and touched God's face.'
Night will be dearer to you than day, since belonging more ex-

clusively to God, for in it you can do nothing but pray, and your senses being delivered from obsessive detail leave your soul more free to join the Lord. This was the time when Jesus loved to pour out his heart before his Father (4) and which all spiritual geniuses have preferred.

'I get up in the middle of the night
   to thank you for your just ordinances (5).'
'In the night I remember your name, Yahweh (6).'
'At night my soul longs for you
   and the spirit within me seeks you (7).'

God delights in rewarding attentive hearts; darkness protects from indiscreet observers. The Bridegroom comes unexpectedly in the darkness (8).

'Open to me, my Sister, my Love (9).'

If your heart is pure and your spirit vigilant, the night will be as luminous for you as day (10), precious as it is the repository of those great memories of God's deeds in human history. Empty of created forms, the night is full of reminders conferring an impressive solemnity on it: the creation of light on the first day (11), and of the luminaries which we today admire just as they issued from the hands of God: the moon and stars (12). In the depths of the night, God spoke to Abraham (13), promising him a posterity from which the Saviour would be born, the fruits of which words are borne in us. The Word took flesh in Mary probably when she was praying at night. 'When peaceful silence lay over all, and night had run the half of her swift course, down from the heavens, from the royal throne, leapt the all-powerful Word into the heart of a doomed land (14).' He was born of her at midnight. The deliverance of the Hebrews from Egyptian bondage – prefiguring our spiritual liberation – took place at night and God ordained that the memory of that night should be perpetuated forever (15). The Church commemorates it in the Easter Vigil. Jesus suffered his agony and was arrested on the night between Maundy Thursday and Good Friday and, though he died in the afternoon, a miraculous darkness enveloped Calvary for the three hours while the tragedy ran its course (16), so that nothing should interpose to distract our faith from concentrating on the sacrifice by which we are saved. Think of that most august of all nights, when Christ left the tomb, alive and glorious.

It is granted to the hermit, night after night, to hear these silent voices and to receive the ever-active grace inherent in these mysteries. Stride by stride, holy scripture traces the progress of God's love advancing on him through the friendly darkness.

In the Sahara, Fr de Foucauld used to bless the insomnia permitting him to make his meditations:

'2 o'clock in the morning. – How good of you, my God, to wake me up! Still six hours left with nothing to do but contemplate you, to stay at your feet, just saying: I love you (17)!'

With thoughts like these, direct your steps towards the hermitage church, through the darkness towards Him who is the centre of salvation-history and who awaits you in the tabernacle. Never be sorry to leave your cell to go to church. The hermit of Tamanrasset was right:

'Being alone in my cell conversing with you in the silence of the night is sweet, my Lord, and you are there as God, as well as by grace! Yet staying in my cell when I could be before the Blessed Sacrament is as though St Mary Magdalen, when you were at Bethany, should have left you on your own . . . to go and think about you alone in her room (18).'

Obedience makes the choice on your behalf; be glad over her choice. The world is plunged in darkness, and there is but one torch: Jesus Christ. 'I am the light of the world (19).' You for your part have no other, for 'the Word (is) the true light that enlightens all men (20).' And that living light is there, in the tabernacle. Do not be one of those who will not receive it (21). Nocturnal adorers are thin on the ground. It was the time which Jesus loved best – yours. He climbed 'into the hills by himself to pray. When evening came, he was there alone (22)'. Today he need not be alone anymore . . .

But night has its terrors too; it too can be a crucible. The desert presses in on the explorer. The hermit has the desert inside him. And so with the night: it is inside you like a yeast leavening the dough of your soul. You only know Jesus Christ by faith. Now faith, to your spirit, is as much darkness as light. And this will make it more painful in the hermitage than elsewhere, since there faith is all you have to live by and there is nothing to distract you from the ordeals which faith imposes on you, nor to help you through the times when God is silent.

For the most part, you are living by that dim light falling from the stars, although you were created for the daylight. You would be more than willing to forsake the earth and its joys if God allowed his glory to filter through, or deliciously fingered the keyboard of your soul. Even if some savoury joy is bestowed on you, it will only be fleeting. God wishes to be believed on his word, without caution or counter-proof, and you are a witness to faith before the world. Your own must be pure of all alloy, with no other support than God's own affirmation. Here you will not know the stimulus of great religious demonstrations, nor the support of preaching given or received, nor the emulation of souls to be guided or comforted. What good you do will be quite unknown to you. God's graces, even special ones, will not perhaps be the kind which you can feel, and you will be reduced to 'wanting to believe', to stumbling along groaning and no longer understanding a thing. 'When I sing the bliss of heaven, the eternal possession of God,' wrote St Teresa of the Child Jesus, 'I feel no joy: for I am merely singing what I want to believe.'

You must 'behave as if' the light were lightening your path: must deepen your faith not by devouring more and more books but by humbly submitting to this withdrawal of light and by putting your whole life, down to its minutest details, under the influence of faith.

No one can give you strength but God, and he is hiding. Without realising this, never will you have clung so fiercely to his sovereign Truth, nor ever given him so precious a gift. He for his part has never been so near you: 'Yahweh has chosen to dwell in the thick cloud (23).'

This painfully 'dark night' will in fact be your light. You will know God by his own knowledge, knowing not what his creation stammers about him but what he himself knows and chooses to reveal. But this will not prevent you, should God cast you into this fearsome crucible, from undergoing the worst that a hermit can undergo as he seems to collapse under the ruins of his dream.

Like Job, you will be impatient for the dawn (24). Soon you will have made more heroic acts of faith than others in a lifetime. . .

All the while you hope, that is, for the coming dawn: for hope is rooted in faith. This may not feel true anymore. But you are a witness to hope too and must not draw it from any other source than God's promise: not from any assurance of your merits or of leading a good life. The conviction that God's gift is freely given must be engraved in your very flesh. In the wine-press of temptation, you will squeeze out the self-confidence filling you, to the last drop. For a while, God will allow you no glimpse of the end of this horrible night and allow you to imagine that, whatever you do, you are doomed to eternal darkness.

It is not certain that you will reach this point. It all depends on the degree of holiness to which God summons you, but it is more than consistent with the eschatological life, to be purged to the depths by this purgatory in advance!

Invisible in the shadow, the Holy Spirit will support you, and your agonised soul will go on hoping against hope, in the invincible conviction of God's faithfulness, he having in the very desert plighted his troth to you (25). 'Yahweh has sworn and will not change his mind (26).' Your own unfaithfulness does not entail unfaithfulness on the Lord's part. When you return repentant to him, you will find him waiting for you with everything which he had promised to give you 'Quick, bring out the best robe, put a ring on his finger and sandals on his feet (27)!'

Of course you know all this already: in the moment of ordeal, the Father's heart, open to all, seems closed to you. Despite all, your soul is 'waiting for Yahweh (28)'. In your desolate state, you will go on repeating:

'For I call to you all day long, knowing how kind you are, Yahweh! Goodness and compassion — Yahweh, remember how long-standing these are with you (29)!'

You will resolve to keep saying this over, for conscience' sake, even

though it were to cost you your life, rather than doubt the word of
God. For darkness hides the bright horizon from us. You will walk
with trembling hand in your heavenly Father's hand.

'I have seized him and I shall not let him go (30).'

Oh, how difficult it is to believe in God's love, when the heavens
seem to be sealed and you have the crushing sense that there is
nothing to be hoped for from him! You have forsaken all with the
intention of living on intimate terms with God. He pretends not so
much as to look at you and makes himself so aloof that you doubt if
he loves you: he who nonetheless is your only Love. Nothing is
heavier to bear than love unacknowledged or scorned. Broken-
heartedly you will reproach the Lord with having deceived you
by making you renounce human love and promising you his friendship, when all he does is to treat you like a slave. You would be
inconsolable over God's coldness, did you not know that 'he had
loved you first'. Otherwise he would be indifferent to you (31).

But he wants you to love him as he deserves: for himself, for his
transcendant lovableness and not primarily for his goodness to you.
You would have a duty to love him, even if there were no return,
since he is Absolute Good. Bear witness before men that God is
worthy of being loved at this degree of disinterestedness.

The desert in its dryness, the night in its annihilation of forms,
speak less of God's generosity than of his transcendant perfection. It
is not sufficient for you to know about this in theory. You have to
experience it and freely yield this homage to love. Were the ordeal
to last too long, you would perish. Humility will save you. Accept
not tasting God's love, you who have savoured the love of creatures
too much; accept walking in darkness without so much as feeling
the fatherly hand bearing you unbeknownst. Guide yourself by his
voice: hear how it resounds from Scripture:

'God is love:
    anyone who lives in love
    lives in God
    and God lives in him (32).'

Do whatever Love commands. Like Job, you can reason: 'Though the Victor may kill me, yet will I hope to justify my conduct before him (33).'

Above all look on yourself as unworthy of any of God's favours: 'Father, I do not deserve to be called your son, treat me as one of your paid servants (34).' Then you will not be disappointed by walking in the common path.

Never turn back. Never turn against your surroundings or the way things are: night is within you and obeys God. Sterile for men, whose activities she brings to a halt, she is ever fertile in the Creator's hands. Before light, there was darkness; from darkness God brought forth the light of day.

'In the dark, it is fine to believe in light,' murmurs Plato. The Lord expects this faith of you. Do not fail him. He who loves you is hiding in the gloom, waiting to meet you there.

'Raise your hands towards the sanctuary,
    bless Yahweh in the watches of the night (36)!'

Part Two

THE MOUNTAIN

'Yahweh is supreme on the heights (1).'

Not without reason is the hermitage usually hidden away up in the mountains. It would of course be quite easy to find an even less accessible desert for people to live hidden in. But this position too has a divine meaning in the world's religious history. It is a favoured place for meetings with God and you must preserve this mystical quality. The solitude of the virgin mountain is a worthy setting for the Lord's great revelations.

It shares the desert's insistence on privation. But as well as this it is a physical sign of the raising of the soul above the hurly-burly of earthly affairs and the sins and pleasures of mankind. It is earth's magnificent aspiration to the purity of heaven. All those who climb its steeps experience and avow the tonic sense of its circumambient virginity, filtering wretched human nature and eliminating the heat of evil passions from it. The inviolable heights speak of God 'supreme on the heights'. The anchorites, even the pagan ones, have always yielded to the lure of the mountain, as though those unsullied peaks were the throne of his glory. Let yourself yield to this enchantment of the spirit: it is no illusion. For you the hermitage will hold the graces of those blessed peaks from which the Lord chooses to address the human heart.

1. Mount Sinai

The transcendence of God

*'Let it be known from east to west
that apart from me there is no one (1).'*

Sinai is the mount of God's transcendence, that attribute of the
Godhead least understood and to which above all the hermit bears
witness before the world. Once you go into the desert, you will no
longer suffer from an atrophied sense of God's transcendence.
Solitude will soon reveal traces of this contemporary taint within
yourself. You will be deeply distressed, if not terrified. Fear of God
is rare. People sin without shame and without much repentance. As
far as repentance goes, you might almost say that the sacrament puts
virtue at a discount: forgiveness is so cheaply obtained!

Take strict note of your inmost reactions to the 'great truths'; you
will then know where you stand. Original sin, death, hell, the Cross
all have an off-putting, old-fashioned ring to them. Serving our
neighbour is more attractive than serving God; often we regard his
salvation more as a benefit for him than as a triumph for the glory of
the Lord. Union with God – to our shame – is more attractive as
the crowning of our own personality than as a disinterested response
to his advances. We have lost the sense of God in exchange for an
erroneous sense of man, by virtue of which man no longer presents

himself as 'nothing' before the Godhead but as 'somebody' whom God has a duty to consider. It would be surprising if this attitude of mind has not contaminated you. It is completely opposite to the monk's. You will have to reverse the perspective.

All lovers of holy scripture are struck by the jealous, often brutal, insistence, in word and deed, with which God asserts his transcendence and emphasises the infinite abyss separating him and his perfections from his creatures. Not as some childish game, to impose on primitive minds, did he manifest himself on Sinai in the impressive apparatus of a theophany — which would have confounded us just as much in the twentieth century.

Pore tirelessly over the Bible, and discover God as he reveals himself to be. Do not contrast the God of love of the New Testament with the terrible God of the Old: this is a false antithesis. There is but one God: he never changes, never contradicts himself. What he was before the incarnation, that he remains. Man it is who has changed. Grown confident thanks to his cultural development, and probably misconstruing God's condescension manifest in the Gospel, he now adopts emancipated, nonchalant attitudes towards God, very alien to the spirit of the Magnificat. Today, man may pay lip-service to his nothingness, but his real preoccupation is with 'developing his personality'. The claims he makes for his 'ego' are insolent.

This attitude is repudiated by the entire eremitical tradition. The constant principle of the eremitical spirit is compunction, and this is impossible without a vividly experienced sense of God's transcendence. This mourning for salvation lost or perpetually endangered seems an anachronism now, as though we were more masters of our eternal destiny or more secure than heretofore; as though offending God had less importance today; as though God now cancelled our sins without requiring regret or reparation.

Without compunction, your hermitage will very soon be lustreless and your life egotistical and useless. Do not be so impertinent as to put yourself on the same level as God. The initiative does not lie with you to talk to him 'face to face, as a man talks to his friend'. That was how God talked to Moses, not the way Moses talked to God (2). When the Most High allows some of his glory to filter through, even the holiest of men tremble in terror: Moses,

Elijah cover their faces with their cloaks (3). Abraham is filled with
dread (4) and realises he is but 'dust and ashes (5)'; Isaiah gives
himself up for lost (6); Daniel falls prostrate on the ground (7); the
very seraphim veil their faces with their wings (8).

'Who can stand his ground before Yahweh,
 this Holy God (9)?'

The advances made by the Incarnate Word should never make us
forget that God is the Holy One, distinct from all creation by his
very nature: his divinity, his glory, his holiness. The contemplative
loves to feed on those inspired passages which, by magnifying the
Sovereign Lord of all things (though his Father too) in his heart and
mind, help him to keep his place.

'I am Yahweh, that is my name,
 I shall not yield my glory to another (10).'

'Be holy because I am holy,
 I, Yahweh, your God (11).'

'Who is like Me?
 I am the first and I am the last,
 there is no god except Me (12).'

'I, I am Yahweh ... I, I am God,
 yes, from eternity I am (13).'

Who would not be impressed with claims like these? All the books
of scripture, above all the Prophets and the Psalms, sing the redoubtable majesty of God, who sits enthroned above the cherubim;
before whom earth trembles, peoples fall prostrate in terror (14) and
the nations are like a drop on the edge of a bucket, like a grain of
dust (15).

This majesty shows itself in the prodigies of his omnipotence, in
the work of creation (16), in the terrifying phenomena which attend
his coming (17).

Jesus in no way palliated the grandeur of God. He contemplated it directly in the beatific vision, and you will easily be able to find reflections of this contemplation in the Gospel. Ponder on the eschatological discourse in St Matthew (18), and above all on the Passion, on the how and wherefore of it. You will get an inkling of what God thinks of sin and hence of how transcendant his holiness is.

The point of departure for great mystical ascents is always the intense activity of the gift of fear. People like insisting on the 'filial' character of this fear, but this presupposes a perfectly clear view of everything, which by definition keeps us in an abyss of nothingness below our heavenly Father. Harmless, artificial insults to your self-esteem are not going to make you humble. Humiliation has its compensations in religion: an 'edifying' acceptance of it raises our prestige and ministers to our vanity. But the Holy Spirit will deprive you of self-esteem from inside, by contrasting God's grandeur and your baseness by his light: to the point perhaps of making you cry for mercy in horror of your abjectness:

'Alas for me, I am lost,
    for I am a man of unclean lips (19)!'

Sin reduces you even lower than your nothingness as a creature:

'In his very servants, God puts no trust,
    even finding fault with his angels.
What then of people who live in houses of clay,
    themselves founded on dust?
They are crushed as easily as a moth,
    one day is enough to grind them to powder (20)!'

You must cultivate an inward sorrow at having displeased Love, who has been so prodigal of himself to you.

Yet try not to project yourself too often on to the screen of your reflections. God himself in his incomparable splendour should occupy the best of the hermit's thoughts.

You are lucky to be nothing, so that God can be all. St Thomas has this magnificent saying, written we may suppose for anchorites:

'Suppose there were one soul in the world who possessed God: that soul would be happy, even though there were no neighbour to love (21).'

The infinite being of God, before whom that of the creature is as though non-existent, will teach you that affections unduly lavished on the latter at the Lord's expense reduce you to nothing, by lowering you to the creaturely level and making you incapable of achieving union with the 'All' and of transforming yourself into Him.

The infinite perfection of God, before which all created perfection reflecting it grows pale, will gradually detach you from the world's delights and make solitude and silence dear to you, where there is none but He.

The incomprehensibility and ineffability of God will settle a deep calm in your soul, making an end of all anxious curiosity. Giving up complicated analyses and many words, you will understand that neither intellectual labours, nor visions, nor exceptional delectations unite you to God, but simple naked faith. And you will love the hours spent in silent, prayerful recollection before the hearth of life and love. You will love to be silent in his presence, since he is beyond all praise. Not knowing him in all his perfection, we cannot praise him as he deserves. Silence is his praise. Job is loquacious to his friends; before God, he keeps quiet: 'I had better lay my finger on my lips (22).'

The sufficiency of God, fulness of Being, of perfection, of holiness, of life, of light, of felicity, will fill you with joy: his bliss will be yours! Know that nothing and no one can add to God's bliss or ever disturb it! Our transgressions offend him but in no way cast a gloom over him. This should not diminish our contrition, but temper it for the soul prone to bitterness.

The worldly man cannot resign himself to being neither necessary nor even useful to God. The contemplative rejoices in the thought. He has but one joy: God's own joy. That is his perpetual ecstasy: he seeks no further satisfaction for himself than this. Ask for the grace to come thus far and boredom will be impossible when you are alone.

The restrained revelation of God's transcendence was what turned Moses's life upside down. The hermit's Sinai is rather than of the

burning bush (23) than of the ten commandments (24). The
mystery of God's grandeur fascinates the solitary and, far from
petrifying him or crushing him, makes his heart cry out in gladness
at being delivered from illusions about himself:

> 'You are the only Holy One,
>   You are the only Lord,
>   You alone are Most High (25).'

Endlessly this hymn rises to his lips:

> 'We praise you — we bless you,
> we adore you — we glorify you
> and we give you thanks for your immense glory (26).'

He is never tired of proclaiming the 'Allness' of God, putting the
hermit where he belongs: nothingness, absolute dependence echoing
the word of the Most High:

> 'Let is be known from east to west
>   that apart from me there is no one (27).'

If modern spirituality lays stress on the immanence of God and
the sweetness of his intimate relationship with man, it cannot,
without tilting into error, ignore the demands of God's
transcendence. Only superficial minds, strangers to the real
problems of the interior life, can suppose that God's mercy has dis-
armed his justice. Mercy consists in this: that to unite a soul to him,
in this world God exercises all rights of justice over that soul, throw-
ing it into the purging fire of ordeals which some theologians consider equivalent to those of purgatory. The passive purification of
the mystics is no joke, any more than the purgatory through which
most of us will have to go. God's holiness does not allow him to unite with any soul burdened by the slightest sin. In this, his mercy too
is transcendent: ours closes its eyes to wrong-doing, God's demands
all the more satisfaction in that it intends to confer more bliss. God's
forgiveness is not a cloak thrown over our uncleanness: all must be
washed, restored, returned to innocence.

The hermit knows this, and his natural apprehension does not stop him from desiring this evidence of God' election. Do not enter the hermitage expecting it to be a place of euphoric happiness. It is a crucible. Called to familiarity with the Lord, you must free yourself from the opaque dross clinging to your soul — clinging more tenaciously than you suspect:

'I shall smelt away your dross in the furnace,
I shall separate you from your base metal (28).'

The crucible is not other than contemplation, testing as it progresses. Experience will teach you how much more demanding perseverance is in frequent, prolonged prayer, than action is.

Passivity under God's industrious hand is repugnant to nature; our faculties fret with impatience. But let God act.

If your sense of God's transcendence were stronger, your taste for contemplation would develop faster. Beg the Lord to grant you this: this is why you are here. With Moses, humbly say to him:

'Please let me see your glory (29).'

God's beauty when revealed to the soul, takes all the colour out of the creation: reflections seduce no more, once the living flame fills the eye:

'The sun will no longer be your light by day
    nor the brightness of the moon shine on you at night;
but Yahweh will be your perpetual light
    and your God will be your splendour (30).'

2. Mount Tabor

The sense of Christ

'For foundation, nobody can lay any other
than the one which has already been laid,
that is JESUS CHRIST (1).'

When God attracts someone into the desert 'to speak to his heart
(2)', it would be astonishing if he were not to grant him some of
those ineffable visitations which have inebriated many a comtemplative. You must leave this entirely to his liberality and think of
yourself *a priori* as unworthy of receiving any favour whatever...
We do not enter the hermitage in search of an experience. God is infinitely higher than his consolations, and only by charity do we
possess him: savour adds nothing to the reality. It depends on his
good pleasure, and you will not force his hand. Only wish him to
unite you to him as much as is possible on earth. Now, says St John
of the Cross:

'Love does not consist in feeling great things but in knowing
great deprivation and great suffering for the Beloved.'

It is very important to understand this from the outset, so as to

avoid mishap by seriously mistaking your direction. The true lesson
of Mount Tabor is not the one people often draw from it.

In the mystery of the transfiguration, the essential thing for the
apostles was not so much having glimpsed Jesus in glory but having
received this command from the very lips of the Father:

'This is my Son, the Beloved ...
    Listen to him ...
And when they raised their eyes, they saw
    nobody but Jesus (3).'

You could hardly define Jesus Christ's place in the hermit's life
better: no longer seeing or hearing anyone but him alone.

As soon as you can, become aware of the links binding you to
him. Many a man repeats St Paul's words: 'For me, life is Christ
(4),' but draws his inspiration from elsewhere. This would be folly
in the hermitage. Beware of sentimentality: the Christ of private
revelations can sometimes undercut the true devotion which he
deserves. The Gospel and St Paul – his most passionate apostle –
will give you the authentic and indispensable 'sense of Christ'.

For you, Christ is more than a channel of life, an intermediary
between the source and your soul: he is the very source of the waters
of life. He invites you: 'If anyone is thirsty, let him come to me and
drink (5).' Before abandoning yourself to his human charm and trying to re-live the scenes of the Gospel, examine what the Father
says. His profoundest interpreter is St Paul. Consider the meaning
of that strange expression:

'For me, life is Christ.'

First of all then, Christ is in himself Life, the increate, substantial,
divine Life (6); then, he is 'the life of all that came to be (7)'; lastly,
he is your life, having only come into the world to give you his (8).

He is your life because he is its cause; he won it for you by his
merits (9) and bestows it on you (10).

He is also your life because he is its object. Grasp the fact that in
the hermitage it is not 'your' life which you have to live, but his.
This postulates great self-abnegation; it is the supreme form of

poverty, allowing you to imitate Jesus's poverty: his human nature
had no other personality than that of the Word. It 'lived God'. You
for your part will retain your human personality but, through your
will to be united with him, you will offer Christ all the activities of a
personality 'divinised' by grace. Thus, you will live 'Him'.

Concentrate your thought, your love, your hope on him. He will
assume complete direction of your life. As a mother says: 'My son is
my whole life', you should say: 'Jesus is my whole life.'

That he should by rights be your all is not a fantasy. Speaking
through St Paul, God says this should be so:

'Christ Jesus . . . has become our wisdom, our righteousness, our
holiness and our freedom (11).'

Before God, you are nothing without him. Ponder often on the
apostle's teaching: you will find great peace of mind in it.

Are you sometimes tormented by those transgressions which,
whether grave or slight, have dug an abyss or cast a coldness
between God and you? No amount of penances could renew the
bonds of friendship, if Jesus Christ had not paid your debts in advance. Insist, like the apostle, on the intentionally personal nature of
Christ's mediation: you are not anonymous among the ranks of the
redeemed:

'Christ came into the world to save sinners. I myself am the
greatest of them; and if mercy has been shown me, it is because
Jesus Christ meant to make me the greatest evidence of his inexhaustible patience for all the other people who would later have to
trust in him to come to eternal life (12).'

The desert will not shield you from all failure. Your daily short-
comings should in no way cast you down or spoil your joy. Listen
to what St John, the great prophet of love, says:

'I am writing this, my children, to stop you sinning; but if
anyone should sin, we have our advocate with the Father, Jesus
Christ, who is righteous; he is the sacrifice that takes our sins away,
and not only ours but those of the whole world (13).'

Better than anyone else, St John knew Jesus's heart and the efficacity of the sacrifice of the cross.

Saving you from false sadness, this doctrine will also preserve you from a mistaken confidence in the personal value of your acts of atonement. Their value lies entirely in the fact that Christ assumes them. In the hermitage, loving is better than self-inflicted debility. Mass offered or heard is of infinitely greater value than any amount of maceration. The Church appeals to Christ's merits, not to ours.

All weakness of yours should produce the reflex action of recourse to the satisfaction made by the Redeemer. Your tears are not what wash you, but Christ's blood, although you should indeed weep at having offended God. To him alone you need to be justified. God will account you justified not by your exact conformity to a code of laws, but by your clinging to and sharing in his righteousness. Do this, so that in looking at you, in you God sees the features of his Son: this is the whole Christian vocation 'intended to reproduce (that) image (14)'.

When you put on the hermit's smock, you were told to put on 'the new man', 'who will', St Paul says, 'progress towards true knowledge, the more he renews himself in the image of his Creator (15)'. Elsewhere, he says more specifically: 'Put on the Lord Jesus Christ (16).' Grasp what is demanded of you.

The desert is not the refuge for some melancholy individual who has made a break with cenobitic society to keep his own identity un-blurred. However alone you may be, you cannot evade the task of stripping yourself to the bone, to transform yourself into the inward likeness of Jesus Christ. Little by little, you will have to reach a point where you think like him, judge like him, love what he loves like him, act with the same intentions as his. You cannot achieve this without massive demolitions. Thus you will allow him to live in you, and will deserve the Father's approval. Only those animated by the Spirit of Jesus will he acknowledge as his sons (17). And this requires a will-to-disappropriation, incompatible with any second-thoughts about preserving your own identity.

By these means you will make yourself holy. The hermit's holiness no more resides in his conscientious practising of a catalogue of virtues than does his righteousness in the exact obser-vance of a code of laws. Be faithful to the Rule: this is a necessary minimum. But do not let yourself become paralysed by the letter. Jesus, who came to complete the Law (18) and whose food was to do the Father's will (19), exercised great freedom of behaviour. His creaturely holiness lay in this last point. What makes you righteous will make you holy: perfectly imitating Jesus, practising virtue because he practised virtue and as he practised virtue, for love of the Father. Your holiness should have the same filial quality of loving alacrity about it, radiating joy and giving the impression that it costs you nothing.

In one sense, this is so. You have found your balance, and balance generates peace. Christ contemplated, loved and imitated, illuminates the mystery of your existence and of the part it plays in God's design. And this is wisdom: knowledge of the why and wherefore. Jesus is the truth (20). He has asked and obtained the spirit of truth for you (21) so that you may be 'consecrated in the truth (22)'.

Jesus Christ is all the hermit's philosophy. With gospel and cross, the hermit knows more than all the philosophers. The profane take him for an uncouth simpleton. 'The language of the cross is madness to those on the road to ruin.' Please God it may always be 'God's power' for you (23). Do not be alarmed if you sometimes find it somewhat unpalatable to commonsense. Only a lengthy apprenticeship to suffering will let you savour the benefits it confers. At first, the cross presents itself as an instrument of torture; it only gradually becomes intelligible by the light of Christ: he has transfigured it.

Frequent Jesus constantly, for he is your all. The hermit lives an 'evangelical life'. How then can he not want to make the Christ of the Gospel live again in his mind and heart? Metaphysics cannot fill the heart. If there are spiritual senses and spiritual feelings, there are also spiritual emotions, confounding the psychologists of the schools but well known to those who live an interior life. You will not follow the Master in vain through every incident of his earthly life, devouring him with the eyes of your heart, observing his attitudes and actions, drinking in his words, sharing his sorrows and joys, praying with him, joining his disciples. Something very different from the platonic sympathy of the textual critic will be born in you. The hermit has to live the friendship extended to him by Christ

(24). There is nothing romantic about this attempt to reconstruct the past. One great principle consecrates it, sending light and joy flooding into our souls:

By his beatific and his infused knowledge, Jesus then knew everything about you: your inmost thoughts, the secret motions of your will, whether for good or ill. On earth he was living with and for you. Twenty centuries later you make actual contact with him who read the mind of Nathanael from afar (25). That Christ should have received more comfort and suffered less is your responsibility.

You know him better than you do your dearest friends. In him, there is no dark, disquieting corner.

Year by year, in the liturgical cycle, the church repeats her pilgrimage to the source of our salvation. Follow her as she discovers Christ in his mysteries. Each of them conveys its own grace to warm the heart and illuminate the mind. Thus, Jesus will become 'someone' very close to you.

And him entire, with his divine transcendence, his lovable human qualities, his saving dominion over your soul, you receive in the eucharist and adore in the tabernacle. How can the hermit imagine himself to be alone in the desert? How can he talk of the desperate monotony of his days?

Live this friendship. It has its conditions for being a consolation; and the first is that it should be a real friendship with enriching and comforting exchanges. You have more to receive than to give! And the gift which the Lord expects from you is your receptiveness. These encounters must become a necessity to you. There are many opportunities for them: the sacraments, visits to church, 'lectio divina', prayer will put you in intimate conversation with Jesus. Be jealous of your solitude: two is company, three is none. Being with Jesus not only excludes pre-occupation with people but undue interest in things. Learn to be content with him. Many people who think they are with him take all comers into their confidence. Jesus is jealous of your confidence. No one else understands you as well as he does, and no one knows like him how to console and help.

So strong a sense of Christ is rare, even in religion. For the hermit it is a vital necessity if he is to persevere and develop.

You will have no regrets over what you have forsaken, once Jesus has taken this place in your existence. Then truly you will share your meal with him (26).

3. The Mount of Olives

The holy will of God

*'Father ... let your will be done,
    not mine (1).'*

In Gethsemane, the saying of Jesus which ought to hold your attention is the one he repeated three times during his agony:

'My Father ... let it be as you, not I, would have it (2).'

This clinging of his human will to God's cost him his bloody sweat (3): even though, throughout his life, he had gladly professed a limitless submissiveness, from which he apparently derived a radiant happiness.

'Here I am, O God, I am coming to do your will (4).'

'My food is to do the will of the One who has sent me, and to complete his work (5).'

'My aim is to do not my own will, but the will of Him who sent me (6).'

'I have come from heaven, not to do my own will, but to do the will of the One who has sent me (7).'

At the supreme moment, Jesus did not retract. But his entire human nature shuddered in legitimate anguish at the demands of a will over the holiness and wisdom of which he entertained no doubt.

The hermit ought often to visit Gethsemane, not so much to comfort Jesus, who probably will not allow our sympathy to afford him any relief, but to learn the secret of perfect obedience to God. Not everything is enchantment in the monastic life. The apostles' hearts and feet were heavy as they climbed the slope of the Mount of Olives, even though Jesus was with them.

The only reason why you come to the hermitage is to know and accomplish God's will for you. Like Moses, beg him to teach you his ways — which are so different from ours:

'If indeed I enjoy your favour,
    please show me your ways,
so that I can understand you
    and enjoy your favour (8).'

A simple, yet redoubtable, prayer: if God hears it, you will enter the royal road of tribulation. Climbing the mountain, you know nothing of what is to come; you have no plans. God has told you:

'Come up to me and stay here,
for me to give you the stone tablets
which I have written for (your) instruction (9).'

Moses did not know what the purport of these instructions would be; nor do you. Past experience has made you familiar with the way the Lord proceeds, yet has told you nothing of his future designs.

'Come up to me. . . ' This is all you know, and you have come. You must be absolutely receptive, absolutely available. At the same instant of the incarnation, Jesus and Mary both uttered the same word of self-abandonment: 'Ecce . . .' 'Here I am (10).' 'I am coming to do your will, O God (11).' It will not be long before you discover how bitter it is to renounce your own.

It will be put to the test with the first steps you take. You were never in doubt that the desert was a land of austerities, but you imagined that there you would be as free as the wild ass (12). The first privation that God's will will impose on you will be the loss of that freedom. Whatever you may think about this at first, this is your opportunity: obedience will save you from straying into spiritual romanticism. Who wanders at random in the wilds is lost. 'The first and most indispensable of things (in the Sahara) is a good guide,' wrote Fr de Foucauld to his sister, recommending her to accept spiritual direction (April 25, 1908). Mountain-climbing requires the same safeguards. On the steppe, there is no 'route leading to a town where you can live (13).' God himself led Israel in the cloud, but his orders were transmitted by Moses (14). The church in her wisdom does not intend the eremitical life not to fall under the common law of religious obedience. You will be tempted to regret this and envy the independent anchoritic life where you might be free of restraints and take short cuts. The illusion is a common one, common too the disillusionment ensuing. Submissiveness in the setting of a hermitage is a safeguard: do not doubt that the Superior is the channel of God's will. The independent hermit is at the mercy of his dreams. He is in danger of baptising his own will as divine. Accept the yoke of obedience joyfully. Accept whatever the law ruling the hermitage, sanctioned as it is by time and experience.

Will this be be something disagreeable? Will the people and usages come up to your dreams? What are dreams worth anyway? Only one thing should concern you: the possibility of a truly eremitical life. If you want peace of mind, pay attention only to what is essential. What is contingent is variable and always defective. What you find, is; what you could wish, would be just as much so. The desert is the land of mirage, that seductive hallucination, the only defect of which is to be unreal. It would be sad if unimportant practices were to make you overlook what is really of value.

The Hebrews could have conquered Canaan in a few weeks. Their murmurings cost them forty years of wandering and not one grumbler entered that land of rest (15).

Nicodemus was right to be astonished: 'How can a grown man be born (16)?' It is not easy to become a child again. Jesus tells us how to do it: 'You must be born from above (17),' that is to say, by judging things not according to the flesh but according to the Spirit. Entering the hermitage is an excellent test: it takes off a man's make-up. Where there are two people, each puts up a facade, creates a *persona* for himself which he exhibits to others and takes seriously himself. Other people's approval means something to him and gives him satisfaction. The hermit has no one with him — except God. What is the good of make-up then? The obligation to be true makes solitude unbearable to many people, but dear to straightforward, courageous souls.

Your reactions to concrete situations will show you in what proportion you are flesh or spirit; if you were a religious already, your reactions would gauge the true extent of the work accomplished.

It needs protracted maturity to become a child again. Then, docility is no longer timid, trustful ignorance but wisdom making a choice. A child's docility is born of a sense of insecurity: the novice's is based on the Gospel: 'Unless you change and become like little children, you will never enter the kingdom of heaven (18).' This is more meritorious: a mature man can no longer believe candidly or without proof in the human superiority of others. In them he reveres a vicarious power, to which their defects do not always do justice but which his faith must keep ever before him. Be lucid, but defer to them. Truth makes us free and maintains a pacific balance.

This submissiveness goes much further than what is called religious obedience. God will exercise the rights of a jealous lover over you, and torment your soul as long as he detects a shadow of autonomy in it. You are neither wise, nor holy, nor almighty; God is all that to an infinite degree. Obedience will lead you to him; there is no other path.

How do you hope to be united to him? Not by giving thought to it. Our minds reduce him to our own stature: beings only enter them as abstract notions. It is depressing to see how powerless the mind is, although we are so proud of it, to seize the true face of the Living God and how it has to dissect his ineffable nature, which is like saying destroy it, before it can form an idea of it. We lack the light of glory.

What Saint-Exupéry says is profoundly true: 'We only see clearly with the heart'. Love is what unites us to God but is defined by identity of wills: 'Idem velle, idem nolle'. By losing itself in God's will, our own grasps and embraces him in his divine being. He and his will are both the same. Ours has then found and quickly run the path to his heart and from this centre contemplates his admirable perfections:

> 'Anybody who receives my commandments and keeps them,
>   that is who loves me;
> and anybody who loves me will be loved by my Father,
> and I shall love him and show myself to him (19).'

Not from afar, not from outside, but inside our soul, through charity become his dwelling:

> 'If anyone loves me he will keep my word,
>   and my Father will love him
>   and we shall come to him
>   and make our home with him (20).'

Then an astonishing change occurs: God for his part performs all the wishes of his slave. Despite his anger, he did not resist the prayer of Abraham (21) or of Moses (22): the reason he gave holds good for all who abandon themselves to him:

> 'Again I shall do what you have asked,
>   because you have won my favour
>   and because I know you by name (23).'

Why this favour, unless because of these great servants' perfect docility?

If you wish to enjoy the peace of the hermitage, be faithful to the duty of improvidence. In this setting, God's will will be made clear to you, day by day, minute by minute. Sometimes you will snort with impatience and curiosity over what the morrow will bring. Train yourself to master the deep-seated taste for starting something new. Your need to act, to create, will often be mortified by the triviality of your daily activities, to the point where you come to regard the two greatest events in the world's daily life as commonplace: Mass and the Office in Choir.

The hermit will remember that everything imposed on him by obedience is a liturgy, that his humblest actions are ordained to the glory of the Lord. In the hermitage, nothing is profane; be careful not to profane yourself by lacking the spirit of faith. By virtue of its consecration, your humble, hidden existence takes on the value of a burnt-offering, and it is no delusion to believe yourself to be a sacrifice of praise, when St Paul expressly commands you to be this:

'I exhort you . . . to offer your living bodies as a holy sacrifice, truly pleasing to God (24).'

Nothing spectacular is likely to be asked of you in doing this. 'Whatever you eat, whatever you drink, whatever you do at all, do it for the glory of God (25)' and do it with a smile: 'Each one should give what he has decided in his own mind, not grudgingly or because he is made to, for God loves a cheerful giver (26).'

Obedience to God is the axis of the history of the intelligent creation. It was the test for the angels, and for Adam. The Incarnation and the Redemption were both acts of supreme obedience (27). Until the coming of Christ, the wills of God and of the chosen people were in conflict. It was easy to foresee who would win: so much the worse for Israel. Yet the Israelites knew that they would lose:

'If you obey me, you of all the nations shall be mine. I shall account you a kingdom of priests, a consecrated nation (28).'

God deplores their fatuous rebelliousness:

'If you had listened to my commandments,
     like a river would your prosperity have been (29)!'

We no longer need the thunders of Sinai, before we yield our freedom up to God. You come to the hermitage out of love and to love. A single saying of Jesus's should be enough for you:

'Shoulder my yoke and learn from me, for I am gentle and humble in heart, and you will find rest for your souls. Yes, my yoke is easy and my burden light (30).'

Even so, your obedience will be under the sign of Gethsemane. It is unlikely that obedience will always be easy for you and never cost you tears. Consent without impatience or obstinacy. 'Ita, Pater', 'Yes, Father (31).' This filial acquiescence is the only sort deserved by God. Obedience is more of a cordial offering than the payment of a debt, though it is that as well.

Pray: centuries of experience have not made you any the wiser. Even submitting to God does not come naturally to you. Like anyone else, the baptised Christian has autocratic instincts, and more than one genuine vocation has foundered on this necessary self-giving.

Often repeat:

'I take delight in your statutes,
    I never forget your words (32)'.
'Direct me in the path of your commandments,
    since I delight in this (33)'.
'Your commandments – which I love – will be my delight (34)'.
'I shall worship as your beloved commandments require
    and shall meditate on your statutes (35)'
'Wide I open my mouth, panting
    eagerly for your commandments (36).'

You are sincere; but are you truthful? The desert will reveal this to you, as it revealed the frailty of the Hebrews. If you come here to flee constraint and go unfettered to God by a way of your choice, you will not persevere in it for long, not so much because people will try to regiment you as because your true guiding lights will soon be quenched. Of the hermit is written, as of Saul:

'You will be told what you have to do (37)'.

In the depths of the Sahara and belonging to no religious family, Fr
de Foucauld obeyed the Abbé Huvelin and the Apostolic Prefect in
minutest detail.

This is the sense in which you have to become a child again. Then
God will be a mother to you. Like a nursling, despite the weary
hours, you will be 'carried' in his arms 'and fondled in (his) lap
(38)'.

4. The Mount of the Beatitudes

Spiritual joy

'... That my own joy may be in you
and your joy be complete (1).'

If you follow Christ closely, he will very soon lead you to the
Mount of the Beatitudes. All he wants of his servant is an open
heart and smiling face:

'The kingdom of God is ... joy in the Holy Spirit (2)'.

Scarcely had he left the desert than 'he climbed the Mount' says St
Matthew, 'sat down and was joined by his disciples (3).' The hermit
should be in the first row, to receive the law of joy proclaimed by
Jesus here, for this is the marrow of his Gospel. It delights the ears
of all, but few live by it. The hermitage will reveal its hidden meaning to you, and to your confusion you will realise that you too had
hitherto failed to grasp the mystery. There is no chance of
equivocating here, nor of subterfuge, nor of turning back. Christ's
word is simple, direct, trenchant and puts you up against the wall.
 Now he tells you how to live in the desert, on pain of dying of
thirst there. The Beatitudes are the gospel of perfection or, if you
prefer, an abridgement of the true imitation of Jesus Christ. Your

baptism has made it your duty to be like him; God can only love you if he discovers his only Son's features in you, however palely etched. The hermitage will help you make them clearer, more quickly, more easily, more completely. St Paul traces God's design for the hermit's whole existence. If he follows that, he cannot go astray. You will often meditate on this, so as not to lose your bearings or grow drowsy:

The Father 'chose us in Christ before the world was made, to be holy and spotless, and to live through love in his presence, determining that we should become his adopted sons, through Jesus Christ, for his own kind purposes, to make us praise the glory of his grace, his free gift to us in the Beloved (4).'

To effect this design, we have not only been given grace but also the Spirit of Jesus. The Spirit of Jesus being an attitude of mind, the Gospel in its entirety teaches you about this. But the kernel of that teaching is concentrated in the Beatitudes. 'Unless you possess the Spirit of Christ, you do not belong to him (5).' How frightful this would be for a hermit!

Poets are bewitched by these comforting aphorisms, not suspecting what painful abnegation they conceal. You will soon realise that literature is not what is at issue, but great deprivation to be achieved: without which it is pure delusion to lay claim to the promised bliss. The Gospel Beatitudes are fed with the sap of the Cross. They run counter to the beatitudes of the world. This fact alone must show you what value you should lay on them.

You cannot understand them, let alone live by them, except by the light and strength dispensed by the Holy Spirit, that living Spirit which animated, inspired and guided Christ (6) and which you too have received (7). He will give you insight into the words of Jesus (8).

'You have only one teacher: Christ,' says St Matthew (9). The hermit will remember this better than anyone. Haven't you deliberately chosen him, by forsaking the world and all its prophets? You have come to him because he has 'the message of eternal life (10).' The monk needs no other wisdom than Christ's. You will have to keep repeating his teaching over, so as to preserve it in its purity, although its intransigence will spare you nothing and you will find people trying to tone down every aspect of it. In time of trouble, you will be tempted to slither towards the facile solutions of the 'right-minded'. The atmosphere of the modern world is saturated with calls to happiness, and Christians too lend an ear to these. The punishment for facile solutions is the stifling of joy.

The hermit is the salt of the earth: woe to him if he loses his savour (11). With St Paul, the only thing he wants to know is 'Jesus as the crucified Christ (12).' Without the sense of Christ, you will have no insight into the Beatitudes. He is, he tells us, the 'truth (13),' the 'light of the world (14)', and whoever follows him 'will not be walking in the dark', will bear much fruit (15) and will have eternal life (16). Whence has he drawn his wisdom? From God himself, whose mouthpiece he is:

'What I for my part speak of
    is what I have seen with my Father (17).'

'My teaching is not from myself,
    it comes from the One who has sent me (18).'

Why, first and foremost, do we seek penance in the hermitage? Without knowing this, you are drawn to it by a thirst for happiness. You cannot live without joy, and if you give up all the joys of earth, you do this out of esteem for the felicity promised by God. To all his commandments, to all our duties, he appends a beatitude:

'How blessed he who takes refuge in God (19).'
'How blessed he who takes pity on the poor (20).'
'How blessed the man who fears God (21).'
    And so forth . . .

All scripture is itself an offer of happiness. The litany of joy has no end. God, who is bliss, radiates bliss on all creatures. Joy is the smile of a good conscience: 'The Kingdom of God,' St Paul perceptively observes, 'is not about eating or drinking this or that; it is concerned with righteousness and peace and joy in the Holy Spirit (22).' After charity, joy is the first-fruit, the sign of his presence and of his fruit-fulness in the individual soul (23).

John the Baptist, while still in his mother's womb, 'leapt for joy

(24)' at the Saviour's approach, and later, that day when he met Christ, he laid aside all sadness (24). Jesus, himself radiant with the bliss of heaven, wished this to be reflected in the souls and on the brows of his disciples:

> 'So that my own joy may be in you
> and your joy be complete (26).'

No one can take that joy away from us (27), since it springs from 'our union with the Father and with his son Jesus Christ (28)'.

Hasn't God himself told us that 'no enjoyment can surpass a cheerful heart (29)?' – and that 'gladness of heart is life to a man (30)?'

The hermitage will give you this, if you make no mistake over its nature and source. It comes down from God and does not rise from creatures. It is 'the fear of the Lord, (which) is happiness and a crown of joyfulness (31)', 'making peace and health flourish (32).'

Far from deadening this happiness, true compunction makes it burn the brighter by faith in God's mercy and in the verities of hope:

> 'I give thanks to you, Yahweh:
> you have been angry with me
> but your anger is appeased
> and now you have comforted me!
>
> See, he is the God of my salvation:
> I have trust now and no fear,
> for Yahweh is my strength and my song,
> he is my salvation!
>
> And you will joyfully draw water
> from the springs of salvation! (33)'

Beware of melancholy. A sullen hermit is a contradiction in terms. Low spirits are the warning signs of a disordered spiritual life. Try and find out what is wrong: either your generosity is at low ebb or you have embraced a state of life for which you are unsuited:

solitude is beyond your means. Often the reason is only a weakening in your self-giving.

Read the Beatitudes again: each is the reward for an act of renunciation. They flower on the ruins of egoism. On the Gospel page, God specifies his highest will for you, teaching you what he means by dying to self. Each Beatitude involves a completely personal reward. Without anything spectacular occurring, each will quietly dig a void within you — one that will make you giddy if you gaze into the abyss rather than at the love of God the excavator. In the interior life, the greatest mistake you can make is to objectify your sufferings, inquisitively analysing them and testing the weight of your crosses. Not that no one can die by inches without being aware of what is going on . . .

Poverty means solitude, silence, abandonment. It means virginity of heart, deprivation of all possessions, even of God's favours in so far as they give delight. It means cordial acceptance of aridity, of darkness, of desolation. It means suffering all this without other people knowing, for the sake of the Beloved, with a generosity which seeks no other reward than that of pleasing him.

Mildness means unfailing patience without and within, a peaceable love of God's constraining will and of his instruments, be they men or things. It means the sincere smile rising from a broken but submissive heart . . .

Affliction means the loving, good-natured 'even so' of a soul under pressure from the criticisms of men, the bruises of life, the purifying activity of God, unguessed at, not understood, not sympathised with by others . . .

Righteousness means the rending desire for God, which he himself makes more intense, to produce wondrous fruit of holiness. It means 'love's wound', allowing no repose, a torment like death to the soul in exile, impatient to see the veil torn aside which now conceals the face of God . . .

Compassion means awareness of human penury, so piercing and so loving as to force you to come to the rescue; a tender compassion for the weakness of others, born of an acute sense of your own, as also of the attitude to sinners shown by God made man. It means an indulgent understanding and forgiving of everything; it means putting people back on their feet with kind words and deeds . . .

Purity means an aversion from evil and ugliness, a filial fear of offending God, a brave effort to atone for your faults, a heroic vigilance to avoid committing new ones, a passion for God's glory ruling your every intention, insistent prayer that our souls may be washed clean of travel-stains ... Peace is the tranquillity of order within and without, in our respect for the true hierarchy of values, in ourselves fulfilling the first three petitions of the Lord's Prayer: that God's name be hallowed, that his kingdom come and that his will be done. It means the coming into our souls of the Kingdom of God ...

Holy persecution means the ordeal of being misunderstood by men, and that worst ordeal of all: of being misunderstood by good men, by those whom we love most. It means accepting this open-heartedly and with unfeigned gratitude to those who thus help us to become detached from self ...

Look at this closely: here we have the programme for true holiness, from which the Beatitudes emerge like mountain peaks, rarely attained but to which we must aspire. Contemporaries have always been impressed by the joyous serenity of the saints: proof that their joy is of a finer essence than that of your average Christian. Joy comes in direct proportion to detachment, and its quality depends on the urgency of our effort to be detached.

If we weep in the wilderness, let it be for joy. With nothing left to encumber him and living outside space and time, the hermit shares the changelessness of God in his eternal bliss. He is already there where 'there is no more death, mourning or sadness, since God himself wipes all tears away (34).'

Yet here-below, this rarely happens altogether. Your joy will normally take refuge at the very tip of your soul, leaving your shoulders to bear the sometimes heavy burden of the monotony of days. There is no anchorite, I think, who never sighed over the habitual grayness of his horizons and the tediousness of his exile.

You will feel more peace than exaltation, more serenity than rapture. Children's joy is demonstrative and noisy, but fleeting and inconstant; it is no conquest, is not rooted in sacrifice. The hermit's serenity is the repose of a heart after a major engagement, of a victorious will laboriously triumphant, of a nature made wise by suffering, of a mind convinced of the vanity of things, of a soul entirely

invaded by God and expecting nothing of anyone but him. This is
not the disenchantment of disillusioning experience, but the consent
of a soul, raised by grace, having brushed the abyss, to the spheres
of faith where it discovers the true nature of all things, no longer being deluded by appearances . . .

You will wonder at and envy the mild tranquillity of aged
ascetics, seemingly unmoved by anything that happens in the world,
as though they had already migrated from our planet.

They have lived their lives, not asking the world for what it cannot give. Christian hope flowers in them in all its splendour, dappled
with joy as earnest of what awaits them: in the words of Jesus:

'Rejoice and be glad,
    for your reward will be great in heaven (35).'

But isn't it great even on earth — this joy rewarding the hermit,
already overwhelmed as he is by divine predilection? Forget the
poverty and harshness of the setting, and contemplate often the
great things wich grace has accomplished in your soul. Can you be
morose when intimate with God, when he is closeted with you in
the secrecy of the inward cell, unveiling all his splendours to you
there?

This is the hermit's song:

'I exult for joy in Yahweh,
    my soul rejoices in my God,
for he has clothed me in the garments of salvation,
    he has wrapped me in the cloak of righteousness
like a bridegroom wearing his wreath,
    like a bride adorned in her jewels . . . (36).'

The flame in your heart sings through your eyes . . .

5. Mount Calvary

Loving the Cross

'So that I can live for God,
I have been crucified with Christ (1).'

The cross dominates the hermitage; it is a warning. Here everything
flowers in the shadow of the Cross; you come to take shelter in its
shadow too. So it is good to concentrate your attention on it. The
world which you have left behind finds it no more acceptable than it
did in the days of St Paul: folly for some, an obstacle for other (2),
and even the people who preach the Cross do it very timidly.

Only by its light does the hermit's life make sense. Christ warns
you:

'If anyone wants to be a follower of mine,
   let him renounce himself
and take up his cross day after day
   and follow me (3).'

You will have to suffer every day, and suffer willingly. You are as
sensitive and weak as any other person, and the prospect is not a
very cheering one. Even for a generous soul, the only attractive
feature of the Cross is its relationship to Jesus.

The Son of God took flesh to suffer. His first conscious act, at the very moment of his conception, was to offer himself as a victim to atone for our sins:

'You who wanted no sacrifice or oblation, prepared a body for me. You took no pleasure in holocausts or sacrifices for sin; then I said, "Here I am, O God! I am coming to obey your will" (4). '

And God's will was that he should suffer and shed every drop of his blood for us, as he himself later said:

'No one takes my life away from me; I lay it down of my own free will . . . This is the command which I have been given by my Father (5).'

Entering entirely into the Father's design and making his will completely conformable to his, he chose suffering positively:

'For the sake of a joy in the future, he endured the cross (6),'

and this entailed a lifetime of toil and suffering: sufferings of body, heart and soul. Everything he had and did was bathed in the bitterness of the Cross.

Thanks to this terrible sacrifice, we are what we supernaturally are, made holy by the offering of Christ's body (7).

The hermit does not need to learn that 'the disciple is not superior to his Teacher, nor the slave to his master (8)'. And were he tempted to forget it, he should listen to what St Peter has to say:

'If, having done what is right, you are made to suffer for it and bear this patiently, this is acceptable to God. Now, this in fact is what you are called to do, since Christ himself suffered for you, leaving you an example so that you could follow in his steps: he having done nothing wrong (9).'

Even were he without guilt, he would still have to follow his Master's example, even though his suffering served no purpose or

person. By structure, the Christian is one crucified, for the reason
given by St Paul:

> 'I have been crucified with Christ;
> and I live now not with my own life
> but with the life of Christ, who lives in me (10).'

and Christ wishes to continue his Passion in his members (11).

Look at yourself: the Cross is deeply etched into your flesh and
soul by all the sacraments, starting with baptism, when you were
signed with the Cross and the words were said:

> 'Receive the sign of the Cross
> on your forehead and in your heart (12).'

This was to keep you safe and also be your programme for life. In
confirmation, the meaning was made all the clearer: the Cross is the
banner under which you fight:

> 'I sign you with the sign of the Cross
> and confirm you with the chrism of salvation (13).'

Eucharist and penance renew this sign, to remind you that
everything in the order of grace comes to you by means of the
Cross; that the Cross is therefore a blessing, though also a burden;
and that you will be judged according to this.

Secular life has its crosses, the hermitage has its; and the desert,
sheltering you from the world, is the chosen land of sacrifice, being
the negative image of Eden. Instead of the garden of delights, the
steppe; instead of leafy trees, the Cross. Man lost himself in the
earthly paradise; he redeems himself in the wilderness. The Cross is
the true tree of life.

Climbing the slope of the hermitage, you ascend your Calvary.
Do not over-dramatise: there is no worse delusion than verbal or
emotional inflation, hiding meagre realities often enough. Many acts
of self-denial are heroic only in imagination, justified by some inaccessible ideal more dreamt than lived. The monk's cross is very
simple and very modest, even if it is heavy. People in the world

think it trifling. They have never tried its weight! In any case you can only feel the weight of your own, since that is the only one that hurts.

How will it be for you? God knows. You will not avoid being pinked by the thousand and one vexations of living under a Rule. This is the most obvious of crosses, and heavy because it arouses no one's interest or compassion; it is the common lot. It is a great relief to share and commiserate over these trials. Try not to do so. But an inner attitude of acceptance and oblation confers great dignity on these trivialities. You would lose much by offering resistance, or even by avowing your distress.

Whatever is physically, morally, spiritually painful, whatever the instrument, be it men, things or events, even if you yourself are the cause, can be treated as a cross for the spirit of faith. All you have to do is accept and offer up the sorry results of your faults or your ineptitudes. 'Happy sin' (felix culpa) is what the Church calls that disastrous weakness of Adam. Lovingly borne, the tiresome consequences of having gone astray are the best penance for this. Do thus, and you will always be at peace.

The renunciations consequent on vows entail a host of different kinds of suffering: the inconvenience of poverty, isolation from creatures, physical and spiritual repugnance at self-discipline. All this, in practice, seems silly or unpleasant. Self-esteem finds little profit in it. Faith however transfigures these tedious activities and assures us of their reverberation in eternity.

It may be that the Lord will make your cross even heavier. There are plenty of ways of testing that wonderful instrument of suffering known as sensitivity, and He who made it can play like a virtuoso on it. The hermit should not get over-wrought at this. Hasn't he come to the desert to be like Christ crucified? God always takes us seriously: sometimes you may feel inclined to reproach him for doing so. A glance at the crucifix, however, will stifle your murmurings, although not necessarily make your sufferings go away.

If you love intensely, you will want to be stretched out on the Cross. This desire is a peak. Do not be sad because you are still a long way from wanting this. It is already something, if you never rebel or run away. Jesus himself did not climb Calvary with triumphal tread. Never take your eyes off him:

'Think,' says St Paul, 'of the way he stood such opposition from
sinners, and then you will not give up for want of courage (14)'.

Beware of developing writer's mania. It is easy writing sublime
thoughts at one's desk. Holy Scripture is more realistic, more in
touch with the poor human heart. The God who inspired the scriptures is the same God who fashioned us, and our complaints made in
loving resignation cannot displease him when addressed to him:

'Come to me, all you who labour and are overburdened, and I
will give you rest (15).'

Our sighs have already touched the heart whence such a saying
springs. If we must never complain about God to men, he allows us
to murmur gentle reproaches to him.

You are to carry your crosses without bragging about them.
Neither the grace supporting you nor the energy of your response
can take away their painful character. Nature will go on whining
and feeling the same repugnance for what is rending and crushing it,
the same desire to flee from what interferes with it. The cross would
no longer be the cross if it ceased to afflict. The spiritual part of your
soul, however, will be able to rejoice over this, although that joy
will not derive from your own resources: it is a gift from God.

The hermit must pray a great deal. Beware of your weakness;
you are no braver than the apostles who took offence at Jesus's
prophecy:

'You will all lose faith in me tonight (16).'

Which indeed happened. Your only assurance is that Jesus will take
pity on you, so that your faith will not fail (17).

Be humble; do not anticipate grace; carry the crosses of
Providence as best you may, before wishing for heavier ones. A distant danger excites no dread; many a man is paralysed when it
draws near!

Even so, ask for the privilege of loving the Cross. Resignation is
the lowest degree of clinging to the will of God. It lacks heat and
drive; it leaves a sour after-taste of regret. Faith in the wisdom,
power and goodness of God has not yet taken possession of the

soul. It is one thing to accept what God wills, another to welcome it and positively will it with him, clearly understanding the good which the Cross confers.

You cannot bestow this dynamic illumination on yourself. Long mediation on the Passion will prepare you for it; incessant prayer and generosity in the sacrifices of the moment will incline the Lord to give you this grace. For a long while however, I suspect, you will harbour a humiliating sense of aversion for the Cross.

At least, do not run away at the first alarm. Do not cry out at the first scratch. Compare your own cross with the sum of suffering inflicted on people in the world in the battle of life. You will blush at your own cowardice. Jesus is the one, not others, to whom you should admit your lack of courage, at least when you absolutely must. The inessential confiding of our trials is often tainted with self-esteem. We look for a human counter-irritant or we seek approval for our impatience, perhaps a bit of admiration for our boldness. Learn to keep quiet about the trials of the moment where other people might be sympathetic. If Christ is truly your friend, he is enough for you. He is conducting the test: do you think other people's interference will please him?

You will keep company with silent, serene souls who have been kneaded by suffering. Never talking about themselves, they are full of sympathetic understanding for others' tears. The great anchorites of the early period were of this sort.

The desert teaches us how to carry our cross alone in the steps of the Lord, as he carried his alone. Simon of Cyrene thought he was helping Jesus, whereas Jesus was in fact transferring strength to Simon. St Benedict has already warned you about this:

'Without anyone else's help . . .
    with the sole strength of your own hand and arm (18).'

It is harsh: but that is the way you have to go. God withdraws his hand proportionately as we rely on man's.

On the Cross, Jesus would accept no help, no relief – not even from his mother. True, you do not have his divine strength, but he is there to sustain you. Your cross is a fraction of his, and he carries the greater part for you.

The Cross is the hermit's daily bread. 'Though without appearance of beauty', wrote Guigo the Carthusian (19), 'so should the truth be adored'. But he carries his cross with such a radiant smile that he seems not to be carrying one at all. His tears are for the Lord who makes them flow:

'Write down my lament yourself,
   list my tears on your parchment,
   my hardships on your scroll (20)!'

6. Mount Carmel

The ways of prayer

'Let wilderness and dry-lands exult,
   let the wasteland rejoice and bloom,
let it bring forth flowers like the jonquil,
   let it rejoice and sing for joy . . .
for the splendour of Carmel is conferred on it (1).'

Mount Carmel – the name means vineyard or orchard – has become the symbol of spiritual ascents, the culmination of which, on the mountain peak, is repose in God in the delights of absolute union. Scripture speaks of Carmel as a fertile, delectable site (2), the charm and fruitfulness of which evoke the Virgin Mary: 'Your head is held high like Carmel (3).' Isaiah vaunts 'the splendour of Carmel (4)'. God himself uses the desolation of Carmel as a prophetic image of the retribution that he holds in store for his faithless people. The magnificent mountain 'will be stripped bare (5),' her peak will dry out (6), all her beauty will wither (7). There is only one mountain to rival Carmel in magnificence: Mount Lebanon (8). The opulence of Carmel represents the soul enjoying the full joy of contemplation.

The centre of interest for the contemplative is the prophetic incident of the little cloud coming at Elijah's prayer to end drought and famine by a life-giving downpour (9). In Elijah's withdrawal to the

torrent of Cherith (10), in the purging of Carmel from the cult of
Baal (11), followed by the life-giving rain (12), there is a striking
prefiguration of the stages by which the hermit ascends the ways of
prayer.

What are you looking for in fleeing from the world and even
from the cenobitic world? Why do you want to live in a cell, seeing
nothing, hearing nothing, saying nothing, if not to be free to make
direct contact with God and converse with him as often and as continuously as is possible for human frailty?

That is what prayer is: a filial interview with God in the self-
abandonment and freedom inspired by love. A cell without prayer is
no more than a gaol or an elderly bachelor's retreat. It is a desert in
the pejorative sense of the word, an arid place where the soul un-
productively deteriorates.

The hermit is the man of prayer. It is a vital necessity for him, a
basic need.

Do not stray down false trails. In your solitude it would be a dis-
aster if you were to become a prayer-wheel, or the talkative advocate of every new cause to hit the headlines. Loving is more prais-
ing than demanding. The Lord's Prayer, the sacrifice of the mass,
the divine office more than fill all the desiderata. It would be sad if
you were to turn your personal meetings with God into business ap-
pointments. Your heart has other aspirations, and God has other
plans for you.

It will take you a long time to grasp him in his reality. That hermit is to be pitied who makes do with other people's shouts of joy,
even though of saints and most sublimely phrased. What he has to
do is himself possess what forces such passionate cries from them.

Nothing is more personal or more impossible to share than true
prayer. It is the language or silent attitude of the individual soul in
the presence of its creator and Father. It is the heart's spontaneous
reaction to being in his presence. Hearts cannot be lent or borrowed.
What other people may think or feel or say may stir our own tor-
por, encourage our timidity, but never give adequate expression to
our own emotions. God shows condescension in the way he interprets our clumsy sincerity, but the truthfulness of our own modes of
expression would give him greater glory. On the human level, there
is that eternal questioning: 'Do you really love me?'

If the hermit is not in love with God, he will never learn how to pray. Leaving his prayer-book aside, he feels completely at a loss and will never risk those long silences in which the soul passively offers itself to the rays of love.

Prayer is of the order of faith. If you seek emotional satisfaction in the vivid awareness of a presence, to swell your breast and accelerate your heart-beat, it will not be long before you take a dislike to prayer. We are only aware of God dwelling in our soul by faith; and so by acts of faith we must proceed. Without this interior confrontation with the Lord, conveying to us what he is and what we are, no prayer is possible. All the truths affecting our relationship with him must, as far as the hermit is concerned, be kept bright and never be allowed to get tarnished.

To this end, the hermit finds 'lectio divina' indispensable. He more than anyone must be aware of God's 'behaviour', to use St Thomas's expression.

No book will instruct him better in this than Holy Scripture; here God tells us about himself and reveals his nature to us. His voice is what you hear. What is more gripping, what is more sweet, than the voice of someone whom we love? It knocks at the door of your heart: 'Open to me (13)!' It 'convulses the steppe (14)'.

The Word made flesh and eucharist which you receive each morning is also the written Word, and he it is in the Bible who floods you with light. He speaks to you of the grandeur of love's beauty, of his goodness, of his plans, of the events which have inclined him towards your nothingness. Theological tracts discourse on an absentee; one word of scripture gives you the sound of a well-loved voice.

May you become a glutton for scripture: another way of saying athirst for God. When you open the Bible, you lay your lips to the source, and 'the source is thirsting to be drunk (15)'.

Read it with a humble, simple heart. Erudition may make you go dry. In it, God speaks to his little ones, to his poor who praise his name (16) and for whom he is preparing a home (17).

Ruminate on those sacred texts which evoke a responsive echo in your own soul. The anchorites of old used to repeat those verses over and over again, in which heaven's light seemed to be concentrated for them. Science would not perhaps have endorsed their ex-

egesis of them, but in them they found an ineffable savour unknown
to the scholars. Their hearts had opened to the Beloved's voice and
the Beloved entered them (18).

Thus the hermit finds food for contemplation. Beg the Lord to
enlighten your mind, for there are those whom conceit blinds and
who have eyes but cannot see with them. You are never to read holy
scripture without first invoking the Holy Spirit. God speaks, but he
it is who also makes himself understood and gives himself to you.
Say:

'Open my eyes, for me to see
    the wonders of your law (19)!'
'Make me understand the import of your precepts,
    so that I can mediate on your wonders (20)!'

Do not read the bible like a history-book or story-book; do not
read it as the fascinating record of a religion. For the hermit, it is the
sacred book in which he must try and grasp what it is that God
wishes to tell him, tell him personally. His soul must always be pure
and free, for fear of being opaque to the radiance of the divine. Let
him repeat to the Lord:

'Preserve me from honouring idols
    but in your power give me life (21)!'

Then too, you must be worthy of having your prayer heard. For
the hermit, almost everything, except God himself, is an idol. He
must be faithful to his interior wilderness. Many people do not
know how to find God. They need something for their
sense-perceptions to feed on, a pabulum of ideas for their minds.
They lash themselves on to speak at length: as though silence were
not the language of the heart:

'When you pray,' Jesus says, 'go into your private room and,
when you have shut your door, pray to your Father who is in that
secret place; and your Father who sees all that is done in secret will
reward you (22)'.

If you are truly detached from everything and constantly oriented towards God by desire, you will not need words. God interprets the intensity of your love: the urgency of your thirst manifests itself in almost physical terms. The attitude of a poor man prostrate in his misery, the stance of a youth gazing silently at his fiancée with burning eyes: these are more eloquent than words:

'Lord, you are aware of all my sighing,
    my groaning never quits your presence (23).'

All your studies ought to concur in heightening this desire. If there are so few contemplatives, isn't this probably because the desire for God is so rare or so weak among many people? Judging by the sacrifices willingly offered, shouldn't the hermit be regarded as someone consumed by this thirst? That is how it should be, and he must put his whole soul into these verses as he sings:

'Like a doe crying out
    for running water,
my soul cries aloud
    for you O God.
My soul is thirsty for God,
    O living God (24)!'

Make sure that your behaviour does not give the lie to what you say. To say things like this to God postulates great abnegation. Train yourself to refuse him nothing. His demands are infinite on those souls whom he summons to follow the ways of prayer. Plenty of people dabble in what one would not dare to call prayer. They are so reticent in giving themselves, so little concerned by what they regard as peccadilloes, so niggardly about sacrifice, so entangled in pseudo-worries, so preoccupied with trivialities. For the contemporary hermit, the hardest thing to accept seems to be not knowing anything more about the world, and persuading himself that it is not indispensable for him to keep abreast of every eddy of thought. Assiduous reading of the daily paper covertly saps the spirit of solitude. And so prayer suffers, and so we find anchorites – professionals at being united to God – who cannot spend thirty minutes in conversation with him, without recourse to a book . . .

Meditate on God's command to the prophet Elijah, indirectly addressed to you too:

'Go away from here, go eastwards and hide in the ravine of the Cherith. . . You can drink the water of the stream and I have ordered the ravens to bring you food there (25).'

This is an order to make a complete break with the world, and entails not knowing what is going on in it. The flight to the east is taking refuge in Jesus Christ, whose name is 'east' (26), who is the cleft in the rock, the craggy retreat where the dove is invited to make her nest (27). God himself will then feed and water the generous soul with the privileged graces of union with him. How much more numerous contemplatives would be if there were more 'pilgrims of the absolute'. Of them, it is written:

'They sate themselves on the riches of your estate,
    you let them drink from your delicious streams;
with you, truly, is the fountain of life,
    in your meadow we shall see the light (28).'

You will certainly shrink momentarily back as you stand on the edge of the abyss. Not without some alarm can we abandon the jealously manipulated controls of our inner world to God. Many people, when they feel they are losing complete control of their activities in prayer, lose their heads and think to bring themselves down to earth again by a stiff stint of study. What in fact they are doing is giving up praying. Accept being bored with God.

Books can teach you little about the ways of contemplation. These are simple and direct: dying to the world and to oneself, living in deepest solitude and deepest recollection, leaving all initiative to God. The rest is up to him. Prepare yourself by brave self--discipline.

Perhaps you will be rapt away to the peak of luxuriant Carmel and from its heights descry that little cloud rising on the horizon and soon to flood your soul with life-giving rain.

The hermit cannot but envy that state of highest union with God, that full union, the nearest thing to what we shall receive in eternity, for which we were originally made.

In the desert, God has marked out no other routes, no other paths than those of prayer (29). Contemplation is an end in itself: it is no less than the highest form of charity; and charity — the theological virtue having God as object — has no utilitarian end for us. So, when genuine, it is inseparable from true holiness, which in turn is only the flowering of this same charity, quickening our practice of all virtues to an heroic degree.

Your desert will then become a meadow. Because you have been faithful, he will keep his promises:

'I shall make rivers well up on barren heights,' says God, 'I shall turn the steppe into a lake and the dry-lands into a fountain ... (30).'
'Let wilderness and dry-lands exult,
    let the wasteland rejoice and bloom,
let it bring forth flowers like the jonquil,
    let it rejoice and sing for joy ...
for the splendour of Carmel is conferred on it (31).'

Your yearning soul will be able to quench her thirst at the torrent of God's delights:

'For water will gush in the desert
    and torrents on the steppe,
the scorched earth will become a lake
    and the parched land produce water-springs (32).'

Part Three

THE TEMPLE

'O Yahweh, we reflect on your love
within your Temple (1).'

The desert turns you inward. You would not be a real hermit if you
did not live in it as in a temple, if you were not to learn how to meet
the Lord in it, in the inmost recesses of your soul. The hermit is not
a vagabond of the steppes. He is the detached, stripped, naked man,
whose dwelling is God Himself, where he is hidden with Jesus
Christ (2).

He no longer belongs to earth, although he has not yet migrated
to the skies. But in faith and love, he already lives as he will live in
eternity. This is why the hermitage is the holiest of places.

'Happy he whom you choose and invite
    to live in your courts!
May we enjoy the beauty of your house,
    the holiness of your temple (3)!'

You who have toiled along the arid track, who have climbed the
jagged mountain, are of those of whom it is written:

'They now stand in front of God's throne and serve him day and
night in his sanctuary; and the One who sits on the throne will
spread his tent over them. They will never hunger or thirst again;
neither the sun nor scorching wind will ever plague them, because
the Lamb who is at the throne will be their shepherd and will lead
them to springs of living water. And God will wipe away all tears
from their eyes (4).'

1. The Cosmic Temple

From God to creature

*'God looked at everything that he had made
and found it very pleasing (1).'*

The desert is always beautiful: the ocean, the sandy or rocky steppe, the chaotic mountains, the mysterious forest, fill us with wondering silence. Instinctively we think of the superhuman genius prodigal of such marvels, of the splendour of the source producing such reflections. Do not despise what God has been pleased to design for you:

'Shedding a thousand graces,
    he passed through the woods in great haste;
    letting his eyes linger on them,
    he left them clothed in a beauty
    reflecting his own face (2),'

sang St John of the Cross.

In the Bible, God lingers to show us the masterpieces of his creation; proudly he displays them like a rippling tapestry, with an abundance of imagery making them even more vivid and spectacular. There is the joyful concert of the morning stars (3), the sea 'leaping tumultuous from the womb' which he confines 'behind closed doors (4)', the 'robe of mist', the envelope of clouds dark as

swaddling-bands (5); dawn seizing the earth by its edges (6); fork-
ed lightning spattering space with sparks (7); rain under which the
earth congeals into a mass and the clods cling together (8).

For him who knows how to look, the planet is still the earthly
paradise. 'The creatures are like a trace of God's footsteps (9).' He
who is infinite beauty has not disdained to illuminate it for us and to
draw our attention to it:

> 'God looked at everything that he had made
> and found it very pleasing (10).'

'Yes,' exclaims the author of the Book of Wisdom, 'you love all
that exists, disliking nothing that you have made; for had you hated
anything, you would not have formed it (11).' God's tenderness ex-
tends to all his works (12). The universe of infinitely large things,
like that of infinitely small ones, is alive with splendours that no eye
but that of the Creator will ever contemplate. The world is his sanctuary, and in it he ordains 'power and beauty (13)'. At the beginning of time, he loved 'to walk in the cool of the day (14)'; it was
the landscape in which he was later to take flesh, and his preserving
activity was lovingly applied, day and night, to maintaining the
brilliance and charm of the world in all its freshness:

> 'How could it remain in existence,
> if you had not willed it (15)?'

The hermitage will offer you the advantage of a fine view. Open
your eyes and admire it, and your heart to give thanks for it. In it,
faith will reveal the infinite, supernatural beauty

> 'of the face of God, whose glance reclothes the world and all the
> heavens with joy and beauty (16).'

Perhaps this will be your sole human joy not to be intermixed with
sadness. Unintelligent creatures are the only ones not to have disappointed their Maker, bowing without fault or resistance to his every
wish. Look at the world; it sings the glory of God (17).

'It cannot see,' says Bossuet, 'it displays itself.
It cannot adore; it incites us to do so.
And what it cannot hear,
it will not suffer us to ignore ... (18).'

To this, the hermit lends both heart and voice:

'Let all creation bless the Lord,
   praise him and magnify him forever (19)!'

And he also knows how to listen. All the works of his hands speak
of him (20). Why close your eyes to the symphony of forms and
colours, your ears to the harmony of sounds, your nose to the perfume of the flowers? They will tell you that God has made them his
messengers, as well as commissioning them to enchant your exile
(21). You are already aware of this:

'Watering the mountains from your rooms aloft,
fully providing the earth
with supplies from your storehouses,
making grass grow for the cattle
and plants for the use of mankind (22).'

Is there a danger that the beauty of things may anchor you to
earth? Look at them as a comtemplative should. The Christian is
taught to discover God in his creation, to see him through it. You
who are taking the direct path to the Lord see his work in him, admire it through him. Your inner eye throws its light on the creation;
the creation does not condition your eye. The blessed ones in heaven
only see our universe in the Creator, and God himself only sees
what is outside himself within himself.

You who are already living the life to come must only admire
things in that relationship uniting each of them to its intelligent, loving source, to Providence, whose fatherly hand dispenses his
blessings on all things (23). God does not disdain, in scripture, to
adorn himself with the splendour of our planetary elements. The
light is 'the cloak' which he wraps brilliantly round him; the clouds

are his 'chariot' and the 'wings of the wind' his courser; the 'thunder' is his voice, the darkness his 'veil' (24).

In thus inspiring the sacred writer, God himself places us on the highest aesthetic plane. Supernatural thought infinitely expands and enhances the charm of forms, colours and sounds, as the echo of a friend's voice enriches the sonorities of his personality to the ears of his friend.

Jesus loved to decipher the divine meaning of nature, by pausing over its more humble wonders, trodden on by less attentive people: the grass clothed by God and the wild flowers more magnificent that Solomon's regalia (25), the reed bowing in the wind (26), refreshing springs (27), the empurpled clouds of evening and morning (28), the countryside rippling at harvest (29), rocky paths (30), lightning cutting through the sky (31), the light sparkling (32), the modest animals of our familiar days delighted him: the hen collecting her chicks under her wings (33), the sparrows fed by God (34), the candid dove (35), the mild and gentle sheep (36) and so forth . . . No trace of beauty left him unmoved. But each wave setting his aesthetic faculties vibrating simultaneously brought him the Father's message, giving everything a profoundly personal application:

'I am the source of living waters . . . (37).'
'I am the light . . . (38).'
'I am the way . . . (39).'
'I am the bread . . . (40).'
'I am the rock . . . (41).'
'I am the door . . . (42).'
'I am the rose of Sharon . . . (43).'

By his own reactions to the beauties of nature, Jesus makes us more aware of them and shows us how we ought to look at them. Before taking flesh, he the eternal wisdom, 'the reflection of the eternal light, untarnished mirror of God's active power, image of his goodness (44)', prepared a temple to be worthy of him: a magnificent setting for the 'countenance' of the Son who is of the substance of the Father (45). We can understand how the radiance of that sublime face, alighting on the creation, has left it altogether clad in beauty (46).

Without regrets for the past or idle reverie, it is no bad thing to revisit in spirit those beauties which it has been given you to see. To-day, nearer to God, it is easy for you to make these pictures pray the hymn which in time past perhaps you could not construe so well. Imitate the lone walker whom the virgin forest inspired to meditate as follows:

'Now is the silent hour, now the time when, face to face with you, I sing the consecration of my life in the silence of unlimited leisure (47).'

Everything is a summons to raise your soul to God: the cherry-tree in flower —

'It is always spring in a soul united to God (48).'

the shades of evening on the ocean —

'What I know about tomorrow is that providence will be up before the sun (49).'

the snowy peaks —

'Men hunger for height and purity (50).'

the willow drooping over the sleeping lake —

'My peace I give you. Do not judge,.but love (51).'

a ray of moonlight on storm-tossed trees —

'Lead, kindly light, amid the encircling gloom,
    lead thou me on;
The night is dark and I am far from home,
    lead thou me on (52).'

water running down a sandy channel into a stone trough –

'The spring is athirst to be drunk (53).'

the turf underfoot –

'To my bare feet, Lord,
   through the surging grass,
grant a clean long stride
   as to you I race (54).'

footsteps in the snow –

'You have given me the strides of a giant
   and ankles which never give way (55).'

a shrub tormented by a squall –

'Pity me, Yahweh, I have no more strength (56).'

The brilliance of the sun, the radiance of the moon, evoke Jesus, the Sun of Righteousness, and the Virgin Mary reflecting his light, her feet resting on the crescent moon.

What will attune your soul to this breathing of the supernatural? Solitude, meditation on the scriptures, a living familiarity with the Christ of the Gospels, constant prayer in the atmosphere of the Lord's Prayer. This is more than poetic self-indulgence – for that would be a waste of the hermit's time if only his instinct for the infinite were trapped and tinkling among finite things . . .

You have the benefit of a garden: do not let it run wild. God has put you in it, as he put Adam in Eden, 'to take care of it (58)'. Think of the hermit's cell as his meeting-place with Christ. The two sisters at Bethany must have decorated their house with flowers to welcome the Master. Do not deprive yourself of this harmless joy. Their varied colours are a feast for eyes and heart.

'I have planted you as a choice vine (59),' your vine will murmur. – 'What could I have done to my vineyard that I have not done (60)?' – 'Listen to what I can teach you,' whispers the fig-tree (61).

— The lily will remind you of Jesus (62) — and the rose of Mary, as will your entire minute domain, being a 'hortus conclusus' (63), to which the bridegroom alone has entry (64). In it, you will observe what modern man observes no more: the creator at work making life more prolific. While gardening, you will feel yourself to be at the mercy of providence, on whom alone depends the good success of your labours.

A range of insects of strange shapes and colours will allow you direct access to the inexhaustible fertility of God's inventive power, as to the prodigality of his gifts. The garden will make you love your cell, and although the hermit is not to feel attachment to place anymore than to anything else, he should even so feel in his cell that he is at the heart of his wilderness, where all his wealth is stored.

Detest luxury and comfort, but love the beautiful in everything; it is a ray of light divine. It is God's beauty, earnest of bliss in heaven, since it is the emanation of all his perfections. The beautiful thrills us into a kind of ecstasy, suspending the din of our inward activity in the silence of admiration; and admiration gives our nature a kind of fulfilment, a restful satiety asking for nothing more. It is the very essence of contemplative adoration.

It will often be granted to you, I suppose, sitting at the door of your cell, like Psichari in the desert, to salute 'the birth of the world' at break of day. You will experience that truly religious emotion, with which Sedia, the Moorish bodyguard, stretched his arms towards the horizon and exclaimed:

'God is Great!'

'His voice was trembling a little, the officer noted. He did not utter another word that morning (65).'

Be the leader of the creation's dawn chorus:

'Praise God in his heavenly temple . . .
Let everything that breathes praise Yahweh (66)!'

2. The Biblical Temple

The hermitage church

'I rejoiced with the people who told me,
   "We shall go into Yahweh's house!"
Yes, my feet were at last
   within the gates of Jerusalem (1)!'

You are seeking God; He too is looking for you. The hermitage is his temple, he is waiting for you there. Better still, he is attracting you there. It does not, fortunately, have the elaborate splendour of Solomon's building (2). The Gospel has already taught us that the greatest riches are poverty: that is the New Testament gold adorning the Holy of Holies where God resides.

There is more here than the luminous glory which of old filled the Tent of Meeting (3) or the Sanctuary in Jerusalem (4); Jesus is living here in the eucharist, and the entire Trinity with him. The desert is the palace of the King of Kings.

Had you ever dreamt of living under his roof and of being his guest at table? Here behold the host, more to be honoured than the convenience or inconvenience of the uses and customs of the community entrusted with it. Men are men the world over. Jesus loved them and surrounded himself with apostles, whose company we should not have liked. Israel did all it could to make itself odious.

Yet the Lord loved Israel to serve him in the temple. The interest of the hermitage does not lie in the charm of its situation but in the presence of a tabernacle. There you are at the peak of the world, at the meeting point of earth and heaven. Your desert is more peopled than it appears, since all heaven resides in it.

You should count nothing too costly to repay the honour done you:

'Far better, one day in your court
   than a thousand in the Graveyard!
to stand at the door of your house, O my God,
   than to live in the Tent of the Wicked One (5)!'

When you see things in this light, their vexatious aspects lose much of their sting. For the Jews, visiting the temple was their supreme joy:

'I rejoiced with the people who told me,
   "We shall go into Yahweh's house (6)!"'

But you are actually at home in it and officiate in it.

More fortunate than the anchorites of the Thebaid, the modern hermit has the eucharist as the focus of his life. The church is the centre of the hermitage, you might say, the reason for it. You do not sanctify the place; the presence of Jesus does this. Who would suppose that, when visiting your solitude? The tourist's homage is misbestowed. Do not make the same mistake yourself. To live here worthily, you need to be purer than the high priest had to be to enter the Holy of Holies (7).

Concentration on the eucharist must become habitual to you. Being shut up in your cell does not exile you from the church. The eyes of the heart can pierce through all walls, and your soul is magnetically drawn to the tabernacle. The temple is where God gives audience to his people. But the interview cannot compare with your meetings with Jesus in the sacrament. At prayer, near the altar, you will not be keeping vigil over a corpse or venerating a relic. At every instant, it is said to you:

'The master is here and wants to see you (8).'

The master, the saviour, the friend, the comforter, the confidant, the teacher, He – the only one – teaching and guiding you, as he himself has said:

'You have only one teacher: the Christ (9).'

You yourself confess as much:

'Lord, who else should we go to? You have the message of eternal life (10).'

God lives in your heart and in your cell. Yet, approaching Jesus in his human nature cannot leave you indifferent. He is the ever-living Gospel, for whose friendship you envy the apostles. You will never have more light thrown on the meaning of the scriptures than by the eucharist. That same divine truth is in the 'letter' as in the 'flesh' under the appearance of 'bread'. As of old, Christ is there, 'teaching the way of God (11)'.
And 'the way' is He Himself:

'I am the way, the truth and the life. No one can come to the Father except through me (12).'

And the Father has thought fit to confirm the truth of this:

'This is my Son, the chosen one. Listen to him (13).'

How fortunate you are to be able to pour out your woes to him who during his life on earth relieved the wretched and is now only a few feet away from you – for your sake! Ought you to have less faith than the woman who was so anxious to touch the fringe of his cloak – you who feed on him every morning (15)?
The hermit is the man of adoration and praise. In confiding her own ministry of prayer to you, the Church intends you to discharge this in front of the blessed sacrament. Some of her prayers only acquire their full sonority when said there:

'You are the Christ, you are the King of Glory,
   You are the Father's everlasting Son (16).'

Although all is in Him and He fills all, God especially wished to be
adored in the Temple.

His presence in the host is the justification for the church's wish.
The church teaches us that no prayer is acceptable to God unless
presented to him by Jesus Christ, the perfect adorer of the Father
and the only one to be heard, for, as St Paul says:

'There is only one mediator between God and mankind, himself
a man, Christ Jesus (17).'

With him at your side, you will all the more insistently ask God to
hear the church's supplications, since these are presented to him
'through Jesus Christ our Lord.'

The liturgy is the prefiguration of that great liturgy in heaven,
described for us in the Book of Revelation (18). The monk already
striving to live the life to come should love this anticipatory liturgy.
The soberer and more lacking in earthly splendour it is, the more in-
sistantly it should invite us to go beyond this world and penetrate
the deeper into the mystery of that eternal adoration. The hermit
loves the bareness and silence of his church. 'Silentium tibi laus.'
Nowhere does he have so keen a sense of having already left this
world.

And this is where, juridically speaking, you actually effected the
break. At the foot of the altar, you pronounced your vows, you
climbed the steps to receive the kiss of peace from Jesus, and in the
communion of his body to receive the reward of your perseverance.
Would it be possible not to think back on this when going to
church; or for the memory to arouse nothing more than that of a
contract drawn in a notary's office? This was the place and the moment when the promise came true:

'I am going to lead you into the desert . . .
I shall betroth myself to you forever,
in tenderness and love and constancy,
and you will know Yahweh (19).'

Do not let the formal beauties of a ritual obscure the living reality for you. Next to the church of your baptism, none should be dearer to you than the one of your profession, which will almost certainly be the one where your mortal remains receive their final blessing: a victim's remains!

Take energetic measures against the stiffening effects of routine. Each morning you are present at the grandest event in the world's day: holy mass. If you are a priest, you actually celebrate it. The sacrifice of the Cross is renewed before your eyes and although Christ is glorious here it is easy for you to remember the last supper and Calvary:

'Every time you eat this bread and drink this cup, you are proclaiming the Lord's death (20).'

Doesn't this say something to your heart, or at least to your faith? Everything you are in the supernatural order, everything you have, everything that eternity has in store for you, has its source and guarantee in this:

'We have been reconciled to God
by the death of his Son (21).'

The pilgrims to Jerusalem dreamed of seeing the animals slaughtered and the smoke rising from the burnt-offerings in the temple. How did this prophetic image compare with its sublime fulfilment?

The hermit should not be bored at mass, nor turn his attention to other devotions. Mass is not a spectacle, not even primarily a prayer. It is a 'sacrificial action', in which everyone, celebrants and congregation, are involved. The Church assigns you an active part in it, and this you must conscientiously discharge. Apart from the daily teaching which she affords you in a choice of scriptural readings, she asks you to unite yourself to the priest when he speaks in your name:

'We offer you . . . we beg you (offerimus) we present you (suscipe Sancta Trinitas) . . . We pray you (te igitur) . . . We venerate (communicantes) . . . This is the offering we present to you, we your servants, and with us your whole family (Hanc igitur) ... We offer you, or they themselves offer you (those with us) this sacrifice of praise, for them and for all whom they love ... (memento).'

Do you think you can decently dissociate yourself from the mystery at the very moment when he is washing your sins away and offering infinitely valuable glory to God on your behalf? What are your paltry solitary prayers or your edifying readings worth, compared to the great prayer of bridegroom and bride united in adoration!

Draw your strength from that, for your hermit's life is a sacrifice. It is not mere pious sentiment to say that the religious is a victim. Every Christian is, by virtue of having been grafted into Christ crucified. We have become:

> 'a single being with Christ,
>   by dying like him (22).'

Why not make a 'mass' of this enforced sacrifice? It is so easy to do this in your solitude! Offered as a victim you already are by your profession: 'Suscipe me ...' 'Receive me ... (23),' body and heart, mind and will. Consecrated you are in the sense that efficacious grace is configuring you to Jesus Christ, to the point when he lives within you (24). You must share his mind, his feelings, his intentions (25). Thus you will be an Act of Thanksgiving, a living 'Te Deum'. Know that every moment, here or there, that tiny drop of water representing you is falling into the chalice to become Christ's Blood.

This will make you think of your countless million brothers in Christ, from whom the Christian anchorite cannot cut himself off.

Even in the hermitage, you are not on your own: the church, where the solitaries gather, is a visible sign of the bonds of grace which unite them. The church is, literally speaking, a hearth of Love, to which all come to warm their charity. Seeing your brothers prostrate round the tabernacle, you will think of the offertory sentence uttered by Solomon when he was dedicating his temple, for does it not sum up your gift and theirs? –

'In honesty of heart. O Lord my God, I have given all this and with joy I have seen your people here offering their gifts as well (26).'

Blessed are you if obedience entrusts you with custody of the tabernacle and care of the Lord's house! Do not resent the time which the church takes from the cell: only be sure to serve with all your heart:

'I rejoiced with the people who told me,
   "We shall go into Yahweh's house!"
Yes, my feet were at last
   within the gates of Jerusalem (27)!'

When the sound of the bell summons you to leave your cell, make a point of looking for a moment or two at the fine group formed by your modest church and the hermitage crouching beside it. Vision of peace! With those pilgrims to the temple, murmur the glad words:

'On behalf of my brothers and friends,
   sincerely I say, "Peace be within you!"
For the sake of the house of Yahweh our God,
   I shall strive for your well-being (28)?'

3. Christ the Temple

At prayer with Jesus

'He went out into the hills to pray,
and he spent the whole night in prayer to God (1).'

Jesus is not only Lord of the temple, he is himself the temple:

'In his body lives the fulness of divinity (2).'

You love 'the house of God', this edifice of stones, speaking to you
of many things. This is the place of audience and public homage.
Become accustomed to seeking God in Jesus, in praying 'through
him, in him, with him (3)'.

The hermit who lives in permanent contact with our Lord, needs
a very lively faith in his divinity, in default of which he will lapse
into carelessness or indifference. Love him with a holy passion,
believe in his goodness, his mercy, his friendship, since he offers you
these (4). You remember that this friendship, of the same order as
that friendship which graces establishes between God and our soul,
has nothing in common with human comradeship.

'I call you friends because I have made known to you everything
that I have learned from my Father (5).'

The apostles saw him eating and drinking (6), tired (7), asleep (8), crying (9), broken with anguish and looking for comfort (10), relaxing with children (11): never did they lose the sense of his impressive transcendence, approaching him with respect mixed with fear: 'Leave me, Lord, I am a sinful man (12).' – 'You are the Christ, the Son of the Living God (13).' St John, who was on more intimate terms with him than any of the others (14), rightly said that everything that he had heard, seen, watched, touched with his hands, was 'the Word of Life (15)'.

Listen to Jesus, 'the holy temple of the Lord' as he affirmed himself to be (16). In him, God receives 'all honour and all glory (17)'. When the hermit is far away from the church, he can always withdraw and find God in the oratory of the heart of Jesus, of which the temple of the Jews and our own churches are figures. Praying 'in him' – what bliss!

The entire history of the temple in the Bible prefigures Christ, 'House of the Father', residence of the Most High, where God henceforth receives us:

'The Word became flesh and lived among us (18).'

That flesh became the Godhead's residence on earth. Looked at like this, Solomon's labours come to life, assuming almost infinite proportions. Jesus is the keystone (19), he is the courtyard to which the gentiles have access in their quest for God; he is the altar of burnt-offerings, himself the altar for his own sacrifice; he is the bronze sea, he the purifying water (20), he the holy place entered by the priests; he is the altar of incense, being prayer incarnate, perfect praise; he is the showbread, being the eucharistic 'bread of life'; he is the lampstand, being the light of the world; he is the Holy of Holies, very God incarnate; he is the Ark of the Tables of the Law, himself the author of Old Law and of New (21); Aaron's rod, he whose priesthood abolished and replaced that of Aaron; he is the manna, whose flesh nourished his faithful people.

The entire majesty of the tri-une Godhead rests in him, revealing itself through the glory of a human nature, the blazing holiness of which appears, through the ministry of angels serving him, by innumerable miracles.

This is the temple where God instructs henceforth. Jesus is the authentic Word of God:

'The One who has sent me is truthful, and what I have learnt from him I declare to the world (22).'

Through Him, the Lord completes his Law:

'I have not come to abolish the Law and the prophets, but to complete them (23).'

Through Him, he reveals himself to us in all his truth: in the unity of his nature and the Trinity of his persons (24).

To God from this temple rises the only homage worthy of him: Jesus is the worshipper, the prayer, the victim without blemish, the only acceptable one, whose sacrifice redeems the world and satisfies all righteousness (25).

No one henceforth has access to God except through him:

'No one can come to the Father except through me (26).'

St Paul expresses this magnificently:

'Through the blood of Jesus we have the right to enter the sanctuary, by a new way which he has opened for us, a living opening through the curtain, that is to say, his body (27).'

However remote your hermitage may be, you can always, at any minute, enter this sanctuary, this 'tabernacle of the Most High'. Happier than the High Priest, for you the Holy of Holies, the heart of Jesus, is ever open. You will only pray well there. Like the apostles, you have to learn how to pray. Jesus alone can teach you.

The hermit has a privileged way of doing this, because of his religious state: he is devoted to the worship of God. He is the man of worship and praise. You suppose you know how to worship; God seeks people who will worship him spiritually, sincerely (28). They are rare. True worship is hard for man, though it ought to be his very breath. Probably you lack a deep sense of the transcendant majesty of God and of your own abysmal nothingness. You are only feebly aware of your absolute dependence on the Creator. Perhaps even the fatherhood of God is only a lifeless concept in your mind.

Look at Jesus, facing his Father: he is the perfect model for the hermit:

'In the morning, long before dawn, he got up and went off to a lonely place and there he prayed (29).'
'He would always go off to some place where he could be alone and pray (30).'
'He went up into the hills by himself to pray. When evening came, he was there alone (31).'
'He went out into the hills to pray, and he spent the whole night in prayer to God (32).'

Gospel in hand, respectfully try to catch the accents of that prayer rising from the wilds: they should be yours.

Jesus contemplates the infinite perfections of his Father, whom he sees face to face, abandoning his heart to the fires of charity. This is 'the eternal life' (33) which his human nature has already begun to live here-below in the beatific vision, and which the hermit vows to approach as near as he may.

Listen to what he says; repeat it after him, so that it may become true for you too:

'Father, I have glorified you on earth (34).'
'I have known you (35).'
'I have made your name known to them and shall continue to make it known (36).'

The divine perfections, as he contemplates them, tear but one word from him, and that conveys all the ecstasy of his soul, so dazzling do they seem to him in the unity and infinity of God:

'Holy Father (37)!'

In them, he reads the whole history of his sublime vocation: his predestination from eternity:

'You loved me before the foundation of the world (38),'

and his ineffable union with the Father:

'I have come from the Father (39).'

Sent by him but never leaving him, he shudders to the very fibres of his being at the thought of his permanence in the Father's breast (40):

'Father, you are in me, I am in you (41).'
'I am in the Father and the Father is in me (42).'

He falls silent, knowing himself to be infinitely loved. Has he not twice at least heard his heavenly Father's voice affirm his love? —

'This is my Son, the Beloved; my favour rests on him (43).'

He leans over the dizzy abyss of these favours, his heart bursting with gratitude. Grace alone can let him appreciate God's liberality without losing his senses: his identity with the Word and his miraculous birth:

'I have come from the Father and come into the world (44).'

his role as head of the human race:

'I am the vine, you are the branches (45),'

giving him the life which he has abundantly received (46) and which he alone can pour out; his authority over the universe:

'I am king (47).'

Isn't he also aware of even being master and dispenser of the treasures of the Godhead? —

'Father ... all you have is mine (48),'

including the Holy Spirit, which he will send us (49)? He sees
himself completing his mission, leading his whole mystical body to
heaven after him and glorying in this final completion of the
Father's will:

> 'Father, I want those whom you have given me
> to be with me where I am,
> so that they may see my glory (50).'

In the loneliness and silence of the hills and with a strength of feeling that the simple words barely betray, Jesus repeats to himself:

> 'The Father loves the Son (51).'

Before this overwhelming love, he worships:

> 'The Father is greater than I (52).'

He is 'the Lord of Heaven and earth (53)'. Before such majesty, he
abases himself, 'he emptied himself', as St Paul was to put it (54).
He abandons himself entirely to the divine will, however exacting it
may prove. This had been his first conscious act at the instant of the
Incarnation:

> 'See ... here I am to do your will (55).'

He knows that this will lead him to death; he loves and wills that
death because by virtue of this men will 'be made holy by the offering of his body (56)'.

As far as he can go down, he does go down, assuming 'the condition of a slave (57)' and 'humbled himself even further, by accepting
death, death on a cross (58)'. To save us, it is true; but above all out
of piety, because his annihilation as creature and as perfect creature
proclaims that God is the only great and necessary being.

In this temple, Jesus is both priest and victim, ceaselessly offering
himself at every instant of his existence:

> 'My food is to do the will of the One who has sent me (59),'

impatient to be sacrificed to the sovereign majesty of God:

'There is a baptism which I must still receive, and how great my distress is until it is over (60)!'

Through this dark door, he knows that he will enter his glory, and his soul exults at the thought of the Father receiving him there to award him his crown:

'Father, I am coming to you (61).'
'I am coming to you now (62).'

Such was Jesus's prayer in the desert, an example for yours. Pure, brief in words, that prayer, but indefinitely prolonged by the echoes which it awakens in the soul.

There is only one prayer exactly corresponding to the aspirations of the hermit's heart: the first three petitions of the Lord's Prayer; though he has no need to elaborate on them anymore than Jesus chose to do on his own behalf or on ours. Keep your imagination unsullied by the gamut of apostolic preoccupations. A film running in your head and relegating God to the background is not worth your taking part in it. Like St Teresa of Lisieux, do good 'without turning back'.

Everything is comprised in the coming of the Kingdom of God on earth, in the universal fulfilment of his will, in the glorification of his name by everyone: the conversion of a people, of an individual, even passing an exam . . .

Preserve the scope of Jesus's prayer, embracing humanity entire. Your prayer loses none of its efficacity because its object is so vast. True charity abhors the particular.

In imitation of Jesus, sing God's praise, abandon yourself to his every wish, let him reign over your mind by faith, over your heart by charity, over your desires by hope, in union with Christ.

Do this through him. He is the only mediator (63): God accepts nothing, neither prayer nor sacrifice, except at Jesus's hands:

'Anything you ask for from the Father, he will grant in my name. Until now you have not asked for anything in my name. Ask and you will receive and so your joy will be complete (64).'

He alone deserves to be heard, because his filial love was perfect (65). You yourself will only be heard in so far as you are united to him.

The hermit who prays with Jesus, sharing his prayer, expands his own heart to the breadth of the Saviour's. He cannot desire a greater prayer-master. Put yourself, as he did, in the presence of transcendant God: this is the only way to acquire humility. This contemplation will immerse you in the truth and make you aware of your nothingness to your sorrow, and of God's grandeur to your jubilation.

In the wonderful temple of the heart of Jesus, you will hear an eternal 'Te Deum': its echo should fill your heart too:

'Holy, Holy, Holy
Lord, Almighty Father,
heaven and earth are filled with your majestic glory (66).'

4. The Marian Temple

Pure capacity for God

*'The Holy Spirit will come over you
and the power of the Most High will cover you
with his shadow (1).'*

'Who is this coming up from the desert
  leaning on her beloved (2)?'

This is no mirage: Mary is truly queen of the desert. To her first of all it was said by God that he would draw her away to speak to her, heart to heart, and in a unique way, since the uncreated Word came down to live in her (3). In solitude, in silence, she conceived in total secrecy. She then returned to the world, without ever being of the world, to give that world her beloved and to assume responsibility for us.

The hermit would not be able to find Jesus, were it not for Mary. She is the desert oasis harbouring the source of refreshing waters. She is also the 'tabernacle of God most high'. One of the greatest graces you can ever receive is to discover the Marian temple and make your way into it to meet Jesus. He is ever 'living in Mary', and you, like the three wise men, will never find one without the other (4).

Remember that Mary is not only God's mother, but yours too.
And in the order of grace you owe her everything. She gave Jesus to
the world and she also gives him to you. She has brought him to
birth in your soul by baptism and there she makes him grow,
fashioning you in his image. Happier than any explorer, you set off
into the desert under the watchful eye of a mother who shows you
what path to take, protects you with her hand and provides for all
your needs: the most imperious of which is your need for God:

'With you, I want nothing else on earth (5).'

She will lead you to him.

Jesus is the light, Mary is the lampstand; Jesus is the manna,
Mary the vessel containing it; Jesus is the incense, Mary the golden
altar bearing it; Jesus is the glowing coal, Mary the thurible in
which he burns; Jesus is the bread of life, Mary the table on which
he is offered to us; Jesus is the God to be worshipped, Mary the
Holy of Holies where he receives our worship.

All this was true physically during the nine months when the Incarnate Word lay in his mother's womb. And this remains true
spiritually, owing to the links of grace uniting Christ and the Virgin,
and because of her vocation as mother of mankind. She is the temple
of the Trinity:

'God being in her (6).'

She is the 'city of God' whose 'gates he prefers to any dwelling in
Jacob (7)', the one which he has chosen and of which he says, 'Here
shall I rest forever, I wanted this and here I shall sit (8),' the mountain which God wanted for his home and where he will reside
forever (9).

Ponder lovingly over how, and to what degree of perfection,
Mary is the temple of God. You are his temple too:

'Don't you realise that you are God's temple and that the Spirit
of God is living inside you (10)?' – 'Your body is the temple of the
Holy Spirit (11).'

This has not always been so, as far as you are concerned; but she was so from the moment of her conception. The Holy Spirit lives in you, thanks to the sanctifying grace which attracts him there with the other two Divine Persons. But he resides in the Virgin as in his own property; since she is the mother of the Incarnate Word, the Spirit of her Son belongs to her as of right, making her his ordinary, privileged sanctuary.

She is the seat of wisdom (sedes sapientiae), not only in the sense that increate wisdom became incarnate in her womb: she stays so after Jesus has been born. The Word by taking her as mother contracted a union with her comparable to marriage. He established a mutual belonging between them, a solidarity meaning that they share everything they have to achieve the work of redemption. With this 'divine marriage', with this collaboration in view, he endowed her with every privilege, making her in body and soul the purest, loveliest temple that ever was: pure because immaculately conceived, lovely because full of grace.

In this temple, God has deposited the treasurers which he intends for us, entrusting their universal dispensation to Mary's maternal care.

Through her, the life of Jesus flows into you. On your perilous desert pilgrimage, you more than anyone need help. You hunger and thirst for the divine. The Church puts these words into Mary's mouth:

'Oh, come to the water, all you who are thirsty.
Even though you have no money, buy and eat (12)!'

Inhale the scent of the incense rising from the sanctuary. A contemplative soul if ever there was one, Mary never left the presence of God. She did not pour herself out in words. She exposed her virgin soul to the warming light of God's love, to be permeated by its rays. Like a mirror with limpidity undimmed by any shadow, she received God's image, to reflect it back in adoration and praise. She gave back in glory what she received in grace:

'Great is the Lord, my soul proclaims,
    with all my heart I exult in God my Saviour (13).'

If you could only be like her: 'pure capacity for God'! Why flee
into the desert, why cut all your moorings, why unplug all aerials,
why raise walls round your solitude, if not to preserve or recover
your virginity of soul? After your baptism, before the created had
had time to break in, one hymn alone rose from your soul: the praise
and love offered by the three Divine Persons to one another. And
this indeed was the song that Mary heard all the time, and its echo
in grace, and the gift welled back to its source in glory:

'Holy is his name (14).'

You must only have one wish: to listen to the eternal 'Gloria'
ringing out in the depths of your soul. And this can only be heard in
purity, silence and peace.

You think that loving God means giving him something? Give
him access, that is all he asks for: for loving God only means offering ourselves to the liberality of his love; it means letting him love
us. Do not say: 'My God, I love you,' but say, 'My God, love me.'
For him, loving means giving, and what he gives is his charity
which allows us to respond to him.

The Virgin Mary exulted in her Magnificat because, 'not being
beneath his notice, the Lord had called her to greatness (15)'.

The desert restores the primacy of the new man; let the new man
sing in you. The simpler the setting of your life and day-to-day occupations, the easier it will be for you to listen for God's voice.

Think about Nazareth: there the mother of God, the queen of
heaven and earth, was only the housewife of a poor family, and her
daily horizon stretched no further than the confines of a village. Yet
she was more than the temple in Jerusalem. She the mystic bride of
the God who was worshipped there. If you could only rise above
the paltriness of your surroundings and live for the great invisble
realities alone! Indifference to the contingent would create an immediate desert zone all round you and what freedom of soul you
would have then!

Mary wanted nothing else but to be the perfect 'handmaid of the
Lord (16)', in the same sense as St Paul loved to call himself a
'slave' (17).

Note the similarity of disposition between the mother and the son. Jesus too came to serve the Father (18) and to become 'a slave' to his will (19). Humility and trustful submission are infallibly and only born of a sense of God and the spirit of adoration. In the desert, man becomes aware of how small and resourceless he is, how much at the mercy of the Creator whom all the elements obey. Like a beggar, he falls silent, throws himself down in his misery and joins his hands in sign of allegiance:

'I raise my eyes to you,
    enthroned in heaven —
like a slave
    eyeing his master's hand (20).'

Despite appearances, the hermit is far from being an independent man. Freed from all and from himself, he abandons himself to God's good pleasure. If you frequent the Virgin Mary, this will be the highest lesson that she will teach you. She says little, but what she says changes the fate of the world and can overturn your existence too. All your wisdom before God is contained in those three words which fell from her lips: 'ecce', 'fiat', 'magnificat'. Your success in the hermitage depends on how these influence you ...

'Here I am': this is the generous offering known as self-abandonment, the unconditional handing over of self, total ignorance about a future known only to God and which he reserves the right to arrange. You must have faith in God's fatherhood. You know enough about his ways to realise how mysterious, 'impenetrable and incomprehensible (21)' they are and how far removed his thoughts are from our thoughts and his ways from our ways (22). You know what the conditions are for anyone what wants to follow the Master:

'If anyone wants to be a follower of mine,
    let him renounce himself —
take up his cross day after day —
    and follow me (23).'

He who would not spare his only Son (24), will not be soft over an adopted one:

'My Father is the vinedresser . . .
Every branch which bears fruit
   he prunes to make it bear much more (25).'

But you are not in doubt about his love. The animal man inside you, however, is afraid; he is doomed by your entering the hermitage. Your holy carelessness fills him with dread, depriving him of all hopes of safety. A death sentence is pronounced over the 'old man' and God will carry it out, you may be sure, in ratio to the generosity of your self-abandonment. Pray for this.

This is a peak which you will not attain on your first day. Firmly say the second petition of the Lord's Prayer: 'Your will be done'; your own will will gradually buck less and less as it is tamed by love.

First train yourself to the 'fiat' to the Lord's positive wishes. You know then when to stop and your efforts are clearly circumscribed. You are spared uncertainty and your only task is to conform. At the Annunciation, the Blessed Virgin undertook a daunting number of sacrifices. But the counterpart was marvellous: in her the Word became flesh. By modest acquiescence she became mother of God and of the human race.

The fruitfulness of our lives depends entirely on acquiescence and renunciation:

'Unless a wheat grain falls on the ground and dies,
   it remains only a single grain;
   but if it dies,
it yields a rich harvest (26).'

Usually resistance to the will of God comes not so much from lack of light as from weakness of charity: God and his will are identical. If you loved him, you would not hesitate.

No one should despise your battles and sufferings. Jesus does not under-value your abnegation, and those who smile about your struggles show that they themselves are unacquainted with self-denial. We sow in tears, but reap with songs of joy (27).

The 'magnificat' swells the heart that loves to the point of self--abandonment. Our Lady of Sorrows is also our Lady of Joys. The atmosphere of the hermitage should be one of peaceful joy. The hermit who refuses God nothing, possesses the wisdom of the saints. He can ignore all knowledge, taking no part whatever in the battle of ideas. He has received the 'Spirit of Wisdom' to guide him (28). Like Mary, he is the seat of wisdom, and like her he thinks that 'God's foolishness is wiser than human wisdom, and God's weakness is stronger than human strength (29)'.

Devotion to the holy will of God will save you from sin, from all spiritual evil. How could the Lord take pleasure in you, if you were in perpetual disagreement with him? In trouble, how could you be a mirror faithfully to reflect his image?

What would the hermit's desert be like, if he could not truly and sincerely say:

'I am my beloved's
   and my beloved is mine (30)?'

Ask him to empty you of self and to expand your capacity for the divine. The Virgin Mary will teach you how to go about this. Listen to her:

'I am the mother of fair love . . .
   come to me . . .
Who listens to me will never have to blush,
   who acts as I dictate will never sin (31).'

5. The Temple of the Church

Being in the world

'Living stones to build a spiritual house (1).'

Though alone, the hermit is not isolated. We define isolation as the absence of living relationships with other people. There is plenty of this. Isolation is inhuman, a sort of damnation. Man cannot endure being treated as though he does not exist and himself sinks to the level of brute beast if he excludes his fellow-men from heart and mind. Invisible links of grace keep the hermit in communion with countless brother-men and, even before God, he is responsible for the whole of mankind.

You cannot find God outside the church of which you are a living member. Be very conscious of this membership, since it justifies your retreat into the desert and makes it fruitful. How can we belong to Christ, without being members of his Body? —

'In his body,' says St Paul, 'lives the fulness of divinity, and in him you too find your own fulfilment: in him who is the head (2).'

The temple of the new dispensation is this: the church united to Christ as, in a body, the trunk is united to the head, receiving all her life from him. And you for your part art a member of this supernatural organism and, through him, 'a member of Christ himself'. God constituted Jesus to be ;head of the Church, which is his body (3)'.

Gladly contemplate Jesus's love for the church: he loves her as a bride:

'He sacrificed himself for her to make her holy, so that when he took her to himself she would be glorious, with no speck or wrinkle or anything like that, but holy and faultless (4).'

He feeds and cares for her (5).

The church, thus personified, is your mother. The hermit's feelings for her should be those of a son. Think of what you owe her: everything in the order of grace has come to you through her, and through her you have access to the Lord. Opening her bosom to you, in baptism she says:

'Enter the house of God,
    to have your part in Christ
    of Life eternal (6).'

And since then, by means of the sacraments, she has lavished her life on you – that is to say, Christ's life. She makes your desert fruitful and provides for your wants. She calms your hunger, quenches your thirst, by the eucharist, of which she is guardian and dispenser. By penance, she binds up your wounds and enriches your soul. Her authority marks out your line of advance. You are not cast haphazard on to the unknown steppe. The church has made all provision for you not to go astray, and for your soul to blossom: close union with her ensures your safety. Day by day, by readings in the divine office and the mass, chosen by her for you from scripture and the Fathers, by long experience of human nature and maternal instinct, she directs your thought and nourishes your mind. Discreetly, tenderly, she leads you by the hand to her bridegroom, who is also yours.

The church is not an allegory. Led by her hierarchy, she is composed of thousands and thousands of faithful people, to all of whom we are joined by real bonds of charity:

'All of us, in union with Christ, form one body, and as parts of it we belong to each other (7).'

Try and grasp what a flux and reflux of benefits and reciprocal duties this represents for each of us. Your solitude is completely guaranteed: these vital exchanges with others take place in God and do not necessitate any direct acquaintanceship with the persons in question. Even so, you do not exist in isolation, since you share in what is most dear and precious contributed by each: that is to say, that charity which is love of God and love of our neighbour. You receive from all, and you give to all. You share the joys and sorrows of all, as they, without knowing you, sympathise with you:

'Each part is equally concerned for all the others. If one part is hurt, all parts are hurt with it. If one part is given special honour, all parts enjoy it (8).'

We are all collaborating in a collective task: the building and adorning of the church, the living temple.

In moments of weariness, when the silence of your cell suddenly terrifies you with its unnerving severity, when you feel that you are a prisoner of the void, think of the communion of saints. This is no myth. Everywhere, throughout the world, in cloisters, in hermitages, countless brothers and sisters, of whom some are saints indeed, are praying and suffering for your perseverance and sanctification. Draw comfort from the thought that you are praying for them. Without ever having met you, they are closer to you than your nearest friends. Your God is theirs, their ideal yours: the same grace quickens you, the same Spirit enlivens you. You attend the same mass, and with the same dispositions receive the same sacrament of the eucharist. You say the same Lord's Prayer, sing the same praises. You have the same mother, Mary. You aspire to the same heaven, and on earth you consent to the same renunciations in order to live by the same supernatural realities. You know the same struggles. And your merits and theirs all fall into that same treasury of the church, to be shared by all. If friendship is a sharing of the wealth of mind and heart, you can count a multitude of friends of all conditions everywhere on earth.

You cannot follow the prayers of the canon of the mass and make your communion attentively every day (9) without feeling yourself to be in heart to heart communion with every member of the church on earth, in heaven and in purgatory; without becoming aware of the obligations which you, like all the rest, must shoulder for infidels and sinners. Every day, thousands of sister-souls say: 'Our Father' with you. 'Being alone with God' can only be understood as an abstention from direct contact with men to keep our faculties available for God. But it would be monstrously un-christian to dissociate ourselves from the mystical body and its present members, or from those who may one day become so.

You bear part-responsibility for the growth and expansion of Christ's mystical body, which will only reach its full and final maturity at the end of the world. We are all involved in 'the work of building up the body of Christ, in which work we all have to achieve unity, so that we become the perfect Man, fully mature with the fulness of Christ himself', as St Paul says (10).

St Peter, lingering over the image of the temple, emphasises that we are its 'living stones' and that we ought to make ourselves available 'for building a spiritual house (11)'. However alone you may be, you have a social role to play, and you cannot opt out of this without betraying the interests of the community and disappointing the church. Each organ has its own function. The ministries are various but all are important before God (12).

The hermit is not called either to govern, or to preach, or to do good works. In absolute anonymity he has to pray, to suffer for his fellow-men and to make sure that the office of prayer and praise is performed on their behalf. For him to stand day and night in the presence of God's august majesty, his purity and the fervour of his charity must make him fit to be an ambassador acceptable to God. Hence, a special obligation lies on him to be holy.

The beauty and spiritual strength of the church at large is made up of the perfection of individuals. St Paul insists on the duty of individual growth, for on this depends the growth of the whole body (13). In this sense, Elizabeth Leseur was right: 'Each soul raising itself, raises the world.' It is not for you to vegetate in an ivory tower; all human cares having been taken from you, you must excel in the duties of your profession.

Your function in the church is that of the heart, seat of the love which makes it beat and which the heart in turn pumps out to the tips of all the other members. Do not fail in this.

Cut off from all, the hermit finds his drive in this doctrine of the mystical body. To live thus, you have no need of newspapers or magazines. Wanting to know about the vicissitudes of the world is more likely to disguise its structure and spiritual functioning for you than to fire your faith. Is it likely that the sorrows of men will have a more productive influence on a contemplative than will the promptings of the love of God? Your job is to offer men to God; others have the job of giving God to men. Stay facing the Lord in an attitude of prayer.

Take this passage from the First Epistle of St Peter particularly to heart (14):

'You too, that holy priesthood offering the spiritual sacrifices which Jesus Christ has made acceptable to God, should be living stones making a spiritual house.'

The whole church, united to her head, constitutes this 'royal priesthood', whose function is 'to proclaim the glory of God (15)'. Each member has to share in this priestly activity, you more than others since officially chosen to perform the ministry of prayer and sacrifice incumbent on the church. These 'spiritual sacrifices' are first and foremost those of adoration, praise and thanksgiving. In solitude, silence and repose of soul, you are in a privileged position, in union with our Lord, to offer God:

'an unending sacrifice of praise' or to use the apostle's striking expression, 'the fruit of lips which confess his name (16)'.

Think what scope and power the hermit's prayer receives by virtue of this duty officially delegated to him by the church. If she is the Body of Christ (17), if she is his beloved bride (18), in whom he finds no fault (19), how willingly — surely — will he not hear her, whether she pleads or whether she breathes out her love for him, through the songs of which you are the singer! To her, the bridegroom says:

'Let me hear your voice,
    for your voice is sweet (20) . . .
    deign to let me hear it . . . (21).'

Prefer liturgical prayer, when it is time for this, to private
devotions. Through your lips, the whole world prays. You make up
for the defection of those who do not pray, and through you the
voice of love drowns that of sin. This is no arbitrary 'socialisation'
of the hermit's way. You would cease to be a Christian, were you to
dissociate yourself from mankind. Like Fr de Foucauld's, your
enclosure is a 'a barrier against the world, but not against love (22)'.
In fact or by rights, all mankind belongs to the mystical body of
Christ, and everything you do for good or ill in the secrecy of your
cell reverberates through the whole organism. Whether the secon-
dary value of each mass, i.e. as the offering of the merits of the
faithful, is greater or less, depends on you.
    Love – if we may put it thus – to the utmost! Charity counts as
the blood of this body:

'The slightest movement of pure love is more useful to the
Church than all other works put together (23).'

If an uneasy feeling of uselessness tempts you to falter, recall Pius
XI's forceful words to the Carthusians:

'Those whose assiduous zeal is devoted to prayer and penance
make a greater contribution to the progress of the church and to the
salvation of mankind than do the labourers employed in cultivating
the Lord's field; for if they were not to call down the abundance of
divine graces to water that field, the labourers of the gospel would
derive a much poorer harvest from their toils . . . If in past ages, the
church had to rely on her anchorites, we need more than ever today
that they should exist and prosper (24).'

Though impalpable, the hermit's presence in the world is like that
of the blessed ones in heaven; it acts effectively on the real needs of
mankind – those of the eternal order, those most important of all:
'What gain is it for a man to win the whole world and ruin his own

life (25)?' By obtaining light for a poor man, by which the latter
can supernaturally love his penury, the hermit is doing infinitely
more than the man who builds the poor man a house to live in.

In the temple of the Church, the hermit stands in the sanctuary,
within immediate reach of the fountain gushing there.

The food is the eucharist. You will not grow if you do not eat. St
Paul says that the whole body and each member (26) receives its
nourishment from the head to achieve its growth in God (27) in
charity (28). This food is the body and blood of Jesus:

'The fact that there is only one bread means that, though there
are many of us, we form a single body because we all have a share in
this one loaf (29).'

Communion will be the great strength and sweet consolation of
your solitude, since it gives you God himself. And thus it draws all
the bonds together, binding you through the church to all souls.
Formed out of thousands and thousands of grains of flour, the host
will remind you of your countless brother-men, all sharing your
'meal', as also of the multitude of those who have disdained their in-
vitations, whose absence you must supply while waiting to obtain
the right for them to sit down at this same table. Often turn your
heart towards the ciborium and call Jesus to you. Spiritual communion is probably the most fruitful form of contact with God
throughout the day; at the same time, it ratifies your membership of
the church and your duty of universal charity.

Your sacrifice is at the service of the Christian community; it is
not an ingrowing asceticism the fruits of which only concern you.
For then you would no longer be a truly 'living sacrifice, holy and
acceptable to God (30)'.

The doctrine of the communion of saints, if you understand it
aright and live it, will keep you from becoming numb. You will consider that behind your walls it is not permissable for you to organise
an existence for yourself of *dolce farniente*. The needs of others' souls
should allow you no rest. With St Paul, reply:

'In my own body I do what I can to make up all that has still to
be undergone by Christ for the sake of his body, the church (31).'

6. The Interior Temple

God's immanence

'Use your body for the glory of God (1).'

The hermit will never read the following words of St Paul without experiencing a thrill of joy:

'Don't you realise that you are God's temple and that the Holy Spirit is living inside you? ... God's temple is sacred, and you are that temple (2).'

'Don't you realise that your body is the temple of the Holy Spirit who is inside you and comes to you from God? That is why you should use your body for the glory of God (3).'

Do not look for God in place or space. Close the eyes of your body, chain up your imagination and go down into yourself: you reach the Holy of Holies where the Holy Spirit dwells.

The moment you were baptised, you became the temple of God: 'I baptise you in the name of the Father and of the Son and of the Holy Spirit (4).' 'Forthwith, the love of God was poured into your heart by the Holy Spirit, which was then given to you (5),' in fulfilment of Jesus's promise:

'If anyone loves me,' that is to say, if he has charity, if he is in a state of grace, 'my Father will love him, and we shall come to him and make our home with him (6).'

You know what this presence means: something quite different from the Creator's presence in his creature. By it, you contract a divine friendship, inducting you into an intimate relationship with the Trinity, now your guest. The hermit sees this indwelling presence of God as the specific personal reason for withdrawing into the desert. He comes here to live this divine truth, to the exclusion of all other occupation. In this, above all, his vocation is an eschatological one: he begins, on earth, in the shadows of faith, by the light of love, what he will be doing for all eternity, where there will only be one temple: God himself. Isn't he already more in God than God in him, by virtue of his willing ascent to the very secret mystery of the relationships between the Father, the Son and the Holy Spirit?

Man is contemplative both by destiny and by nature:

'Eternal life is this,' Jesus teaches: 'to know you, the only true God, and Jesus Christ whom you have sent (7)'.

but to know this with an awareness participating in God's own awareness, seeing him face to face in the beatific vision. To know him is the supreme objective of our minds, which are made for truth. To love him is the sum of our will, which is greedy for the Good. Our earthly condition interposes a whole gamut of partial truths and fragmentary goods between God and us and, although these ought to help us to return to their source, as often as not they divert us from it by reason of the undue value which we place on them.

Isn't it strange that man, designed to flourish in contemplation dilating him to the proportions of God, should prefer activities which throw him back on himself in his will-to-achieve? It is easier to act than to pray: here the initiative belongs to God, there it is our own, and we do not enjoy giving our freedom up – even for the Lord's benefit. This presents a real puzzle to faith: that most people dislike contemplation and regard it as the idle Christian's pastime.

Indifference to God's presence in the soul is an insult, and sin a sort of sacrilege:

'If anyone destroys the temple of God,
    God will destroy him (8).'

The hermit has abandandoned everything to become fixed in this presence. With all earthly avenues closed, he dares advance his claim to be a 'fellow-citizen with the saints (9)'. His Christian profession and formal vocation summoning him to solitude are the basis for his claim. There, if he understands it aright, there is only one temple, body and soul (10). The disciplining of his senses and 'the enslavement of his flesh' will take on a higher meaning than that of a laboriously sustained effort of self-mastery; the body, for its part, is a valuable stone which must be cut and polished to form part of the church now in process of being built (11). Far from debasing it, the hermit will treat it with respect, mindful of the role assigned to it by the liturgy. The liturgy lays down a detailed ritual, governing and ennobling the attitudes and functions of each limb in the way it should play its part in prayer and sacrifice.

The dignity of the body is primarily derived from the soul which animates it, substantial union with which allows it to share the honour of being the dwelling-place of the Most High. Our more enlightened theology of the body no longer permits us to treat it in the squalid way affected by the hermits of old. Baptism has washed it in purifying water, the priest has signed it with the Cross and anointed it with holy chrism, and eucharistic communion makes it a living ciborium. When it dies, the church censes it and carries it in triumph. For isn't it the 'temple of the Holy Spirit (12)'?

Act then, so that it becomes what it is. Thanks to the proper functioning of its organs, the body makes it possible for the soul consciously to enjoy the presence of God within her. Be careful that indiscreet severity does not make you unable to maintain your prolonged conversation with the Lord within you. If Mary Magdalen had been suffering from migraine, the conversation at Bethany would have been spoilt.

You cannot consider what is taking place inside you, without a sense of joy. While you are eating, while you are relaxing, while you are asleep, the Father is begetting his Divine Son in your soul. His word is coming true every second:

'Today I have begotten you (13).'

Try by faith to perceive something of these exchanges of love and praise between the Divine Persons, for of such is the life and glory of the Trinity now irradiating your own soul.

The 'Gloria Patri' punctuating your psalmody is only an echo, though a most faithful one, of the praise which Father, Son and Holy Spirit render to one another.

The Father's glory is his Son, receiving and perfectly reflecting all his perfections. He is his inward Word, his song. He praises him as the source of all divine excellences, the 'beginning'.

The Son's glory is the Father, bearing witness, while begetting him as perfect as himself, to his transcendant beauty.

The Holy Spirit's glory is the mutual joy of the Father and the Son, whose substantial kiss he is.

Ask him to let you be more sensitive to this magnificent hymn, summing up all other religious acts, that is to say, every act of your hermit-life, since all are directed to glorifying God.

As you repeat this ineffable 'Gloria' with the Trinity, you share the Trinity's bliss. This is the supreme consolation the desert can offer, and the only one the hermit may legitimately covet. For one drop of this gladness, the saints have forsaken everything. In your retreat, try and put your heart in tune with God's heart, so that your joy consists in whatever gives joy to each of the Divine Persons.

The Father's joy is his Son. And is entirely expressed in the begetting word:

'Filius meus es tu' ... 'You are my son (14),'

the Word like him in all respects, his living image, to whom he is drawn in all love and who returns that love in equal degree.

The Son's joy is his Father, from whom he receives all that he is: the Father who at a stroke transfers all his fruitfulness to him, sharing his divine nature with him and all his own perfections; the Son's bliss it is to be 'nearest to the Father's heart (15)' and to love him with infinite gratitude super-added.

The Holy Spirit's joy is the very joy of Father and Son fusing together in this third person. Being the substantial love of the first two persons, the Holy Spirit is called the heart of God. He is a song, a divine festival, the sublime vibrancy of Love. In God, he is the hearth of joy and bliss.

No human joy can compare with the bliss of the Godhead. But the hermit knows that this is not some alien wonder, still less a proposition to be worked out from books, not a distant spectacle, the inaccessible splendour of which would only make his own Thebaid the more dismal.

Temple of the Godhead, the heart of God beats in you. In the heart of your soul, the marvellous life of the Trinity is taking place. Remember these words of a theologian:

'At this very moment, which I am wasting on trifles, Almighty God is busy within me, bringing his co-eternal Son to birth (16).'

You are God's adopted child (17) and hence you live in the bosom of the divine family, where Jesus sponsors you and trains you:

'Father, I want those whom you have given me to be with me where I am (18).'

And where is Jesus? 'In the Father's bosom(19).' Faith, charity and sharing in the awareness which God has of himself, in the love which he bears to himself, plunge you into the living current of circumincession. Isn't that the meaning of Christ's prayer:

'That they may be one as we are one,
    I in them and you in me (20).'

This, then, will be your interior life in the hermitage: as continuously as you can, you will associate your personal acts with the three divine persons' song of glory and love, so that your own acts, assumed by Jesus Christ, may rise, infinitely precious, to God. Depending on the dictates of the moment, unite with the Father in celebrating the glory of the Son, with the Son in exalting the glory of the Father, with the Holy Spirit in tasting the joy of the Trinity entire.

This can only be consistently done in lively faith, bareness of mind and silence. No creature, no image will help you. Though created things reveal God's nature to you, they tell you nothing about the way he lives. To grasp this, you must go beyond terrestrial things and forget them. The day when you feel a genuine desire forcing you to sigh:

'Like a doe crying out
    for running water,
my soul cries aloud
    for you, O God.
My soul is thirsty for God,
    O Living God (21),'

you will know that God is knocking at your door and wants to 'share your meal (22)'. That will be the Spirit of the Son, whom God has sent into your heart, crying 'Abba, Father (23)', and with ineffable groans begging on your behalf for 'those things which are according to the mind of God (24)', which for you means perfect union with him.

Such is the last why and wherefore of the hermit's detachment: why he follows the Lord's advice to the letter, 'by retiring into his cells, shutting the door and praying to his Father, who is there in that secret place (25)'. He does this physically, and even more so spiritually, by intense recollectedness in the interior cell which the hermitage affords him.

Have no scruples about only devoting little time to 'devotions', about not overloading yourself with particular intentions: the official prayer of the church provides for all, and the honour which the church renders to the saints in her offices and the apostolic efficacity of her supplication, far exceed any private homage or intercession of yours. Jesus in heaven, says the Epistle to the Hebrews, 'is living forever to intercede on our behalf (26)'. He does this, not by formulated requests, but by the sole presence of the glorious scars of his passion: the reminders of his love and obedience. By virtue of its consecrated state and fervent charity, your whole existence pleads that God's name should be hallowed, that his kingdom should come and that his will be done.

The hermit may rightly consider himself as already taking part in the glorious liturgy of eternity, described in Revelation. He already has his place among the myriads of myriads, among the thousands of thousands of angels and saints assembled round the throne of God, 'shouting: to the One who is sitting on the throne and to the Lamb, be all praise, honour, glory and power for ever and ever (27)'.

If your liturgy is made as simple as it can be, if you are allowed long hours of solitude and leisure, this is to let you soul, set free of all constraints, anticipate as far as may be what our eternal life will be. For all this, do not hope never again to experience the heaviness and boredom of desolate prayer. The festival is all for faith and love. The joy is God's, not yours – as regards what is felt.

However unhappy you may be, adoration – for egoism can play no part in this – will always be a blessed release for you from self-concern. God's bliss will be your joy: this is the supreme disinterestedness of true charity.

May the lovely acclamations of the 'Gloria in excelsis' ring out unceasingly in the temple of your soul:

'Glory to God in highest Heaven ...
We praise you, we bless you,
we adore you, we glorify you,
and we give you thanks
for your immense glory ... '

Since no other voice is raised in the desert but yours, at least there will be one place on earth where God is worshipped purely ...

Epilogue

THE CELL

'He has taken me into his cellar
and the banner he raises over me
is love (1).'

Of all these splendours, the first weeks in your cell will reveal very little, perhaps nothing. Humbly accept the boredom, the pacing to and fro. Your heart is still raw from everything which you have left behind, and the whitewashed walls are bare except for a crucifix and a madonna. There is still too much tumult in your imagination and emotions for you to be enthralled by the Invisible. You used to dream of this little house, sister to the one (it would seem) where the *Imitation of Christ* was written. Now you are in it and you shudder. You would like to run away.

Be patient, pray, quickly devise a round of activities, reading, short studies in the Bible or any other spiritual subject which attracts you. You will gradually discover and come to savour the delights of the cell. Those who have celebrated these in moving phrases echoing down the centuries were not novices, believe me, and like you had first experienced its austerity.

The hermit's cell is a dwelling unique of its kind. It is neither a clergyman's office, nor the cell of a Jesuit or a mendicant. The solitary sleeps in it, works in it, eats and relaxes in it. But its distinguishing characteristic is that it is his entire universe. Apart from his visits to the church, he must seek nothing outside it. For him, everything is contained within this minute enclosure.

All the riches of the desert, of the mountain and of the temple are so concentrated for the hermit here that if he leaves without some reason dictated by obedience, he instantly loses all. He finds nothing outside; what nourishes other people's piety is of no use to him. The hermit is tied to his cell for his soul's subsistence.

The cell is a shelter from the miasmas of the world, a holy place where the Lord pays secret visits to the soul and where the soul waits in recollectedness for him, having scorned all else. It is the 'wine-cellar (2)' into which he takes his beloved, to make her drunk with his presence and his presents.

It would be a profanation to abandon yourself to futile activities there. There God grants audience to the solitary soul. On the confines of earthly life, released from those contingencies under which most souls athirst for God must groan since victims of life's harsh conditions, the hermit begins his eternity rejoicing in the Lord.

If you are generous, little by little you will see the divine world emerging from the shadows. You have been living in it unawares, the hurly-burly of the world not having allowed it to be seen. You then in your turn will wonderingly discover that you are never less alone than when you are alone . . .

References

PART ONE: THE DESERT

1 Ho 2:16

Chapter One
1 Ps 136:16
2 Ex 14:11; 16:3; Nb 14:2, &c.
3 Gn 12:1-4
4 2nd Sermon: Assumption
5 Ex 19:4
6 Ho 2:16–18
7 Gn 1:2
8 Jr 2:6
9 Br Milad Aissa, Little Brother of Jesus: Introd. to the Spiritual Works of Fr de Foucauld. Edit. Seuil, p.20
10 Rule of St Benedict, ch.1.
11 Gn 21
12 1 K 19
13 1 K 19:12
14 Nb 12:7–8
15 Maxim 147. Ed. Lucien (Seuil)
16 Jn 6:44
17 Ex 16
18 Ex 40:36–38
19 Ex 20
20 Ex 19
21 Ex 24–31
22 Nb 20:1–11
23 Ps 42:1–2
24 Ex 40:36–38
25 Dt 32:10–12
26 Dt 32:20

Chapter Two
1 Jn 1:38–39
2 Jn 15:16
3 Jr 1:5
4 Is 49:1; cf. Ga 1:15

5 Mt 4
6 Is 49:2
7 Is 66:12–13
8 Is 66:14
9 Ep 1:4
10 Ep 6:3
11 Sg 6:1–3
12 Mt 11:11
13 Jn 5:35
14 Rv 22:17
15 Jn 1:23
16 Jn 3:30
17 Ga 2:20
18 Mt 5:16
19 Rm 8:29
20 2 Co 4:10
21 2 Co 3:18
22 Jn 1:5
23 Jn 12:32
24 Mt 11:9
25 Mt 11:11
26 Cf. 2 Co 1:5
27 Ch. Lk 2:29–32
28 Maxim 165

Chapter Three
1 Mk 1:12–13
2 Mk 1:10
3 Mk 1:12
4 Mk 1:11
5 The Lord, I Baptism & Temptation 37.
6 Address to the Congress for Oriental Monastic Studies, April 1958.
7 1 Jn 1:5
8 1 Jn 4:8
9 Ne 4:12

10 Problems of Spiritual Life.
11 Mt 12:43
12 4:1
13 Rule, ch.1.
14 Ps 34:8
15 Mt 4:6
16 Lk 12:37

Chapter Four
1 Lk 7:47
2 Lk 15:4–7
3 1 Jn 4:10
5 Pr 15:3
6 Ps 139:16
7 Cf. Rm 9:14–24
8 Jn 1:48
9 Lk 7:48–50
10 Lk 10:39
11 Is 1:18
12 Is 38:17
13 Jr 31:20
14 Letter to L. Massignon, Dec.3, 1909, Spiritual Writings (Seuil).
15 Is 44:21–22
16 Is 45:23
17 Rm 8:32
18 Ga 2:20
19 Mt 27:46
21 Rv 3:20
22 Ph 3:20–21
23 Col 3: 1–4
24 Ho 9:10

Chapter Five
1 Ph 1:21
2 Ga 1:15–17

3 Cf. 1 Co 7:22; Ga 1:10; Ep 6:6
4 Cf. Col 4:3; Ep 3:1; Ph 1:9
5 Ac 9:5
6 1 Co 15:10
7 Cf. 2 Co 11
8 Cf. 2 Co 6
9 Col 1:26
10 Ga 1:17
11 Ac 9:4
12 2 Co 5:14
13 1 Co 16:22
14 Rm 8:35
15 Mt 5:48
16 Col 1:15
17 Ep 1:4–5
18 1 Co 12:27
19 1 Co 12:13
20 Ga 2:20
21 Ph 3:20
22 Ep 2:19
23 Col 3:1–3
24 Ep 2:1–7
25 Ga 2:20
26 Ga 6:17
27 1 Co 9:27
28 Ga 2:19
29 Ga 6:14
30 Ph 3:8
31 1 Co 9:26
32 Ph 3:5
33 2 Co 12:2
34 Ph 1:23
35 Ep 3:3
36 Ep 3:8–9
37 Ep 1:10
38 1 Co 15:25
39 Ep 2:7
40 Ep 3:8–9
41 Rm 8:37
42 Ep 4: 22–24
43 Rm 13:14
44 2 Tm 1:12
45 Ph 4:13
46 2 Tm 4:7

Chapter Six
1 Ps 139:12
2 Ba 3:34–39
3 Ps 19:1
4 Lk 6:12
5 Ps 119:62
6 Ps 119:55
7 Is 26:9
8 Mt 25:6
9 Sg 5:2
10 Ps 139:12
11 Gn 1:4
12 Gn 1:16
13 Gn 15:5
14 Ws 18:14–15
15 Ex 12:42
16 Mt 27:45
17 New Spiritual Writings, page 112
18 Spiritual Writings, page 69
19 Jn 8:12;9:5; 12:46
20 Jn 1:9
21 Jn1:11
22 Mt 14:23
23 1 K 8:12
24 Jb 17:12
25 Ho 2:22
26 Ps 110:4
27 Lk 15:22

28 Ps 33:20
29 Ps 25:5–6
30 Sg 3:4
31 1 Jn 4:10
32 1 Jn 4:16

33 Jb 13:15
34 Lk 15:19
35 Gn 1:1
36 Ps 134:2

PART TWO: THE MOUNTAIN

1 Ps 93:4 (LXX)

Chapter One
 1 Is 45:6
 2 Ex 33:11
 3 Ex 3:6; 33:23; 1 K 19:13
 4 Gn 15:12
 5 Gn 18:27
 6 Is 6:5
 7 Dn 10:8–9
 8 Is 6:2
 9 1 S 6:20
10 Is 42:8
11 Lv 11:44; 20:26
12 Is 44:6
13 Is 43:11–12
14 Cf. Ps 99:1–5
15 Is 40:15
16 Is 45:11–12
17 Ps 77:16–19;
     Hab 3:3–6 &c
18 24:1f
19 Is 6:5
20 Jb 4:17–20
21 S.T.I. II:4.8.3
22 40:4
23 Ex 3

24 Ex 19
25 Gloria
26 Gloria
27 Is 45:6
28 Is 1:25
29 Ex 33:18
30 Is 60:19

Chapter Two
 1 1 Co 3:11
 2 Ho 1:16
 3 Mt 17:5–7
 4 Ph 1:21
 5 Jn 7:37; 4:10–14;
     Is 55:1–3
 6 Jn 14:6: 5:26; 1:4
 7 Jn 1:4; 11:25; 14:6
 8 Jn 10:10; 5:40; 6:33
 9 Heb 9:12
10 Rm 6:23; 1 Jn 2:25;
     5:11–12
11 1 Co 1:30
12 1 Tm 1:15–16
13 1 Jn 2:1–2
14 Rm 8:29
15 Col 3:10
16 Rm 13:14

17 Rm 8:14
18 Mt 5:17
19 Jn 4:34
20 Jn 14:6
21 Jn 14:16–17; 15:26
22 Jn 17:17
23 1 Co 1:18
24 Jn 15:15
25 Jn 1:48
26 Rv 3:20

Chapter Three
 1 Lk 22:42
 2 Mt 26:36–44
 3 Lk 22:44
 4 Heb 10:7
 5 Jn 4:34
 6 Jn 5:30
 7 Jn 6:38
 8 Ex 33:13
 9 Ex 24:12
10 Lk 1:38; Heb 10:7
11 Heb 10:9
12 Jb 39:5
13 Ps 107:4
14 Nb 9:23
15 Nb 14:23–26; Dt
    1:34–40
16 Jn 3:4
17 Jn 3:7
18 Mt 18:3
19 Jn 14:21
20 Jn 14:23
21 Gn 18:22–33
22 Ex 32:14; 33:17f
23 Ibid.
24 Rm 12:1
25 1 Co 10:31

26 2 Co 9:7
27 Cf. Heb 7:7; Ph 2:8
28 Ex 19:5–6
29 Is 48:18
30 Mt 11:26
32 Ps 119:16
33 Ps 119:35
34 Ps 119:47
35 Ps 119:48
36 Ps 119:131
37 Ac 9:6
38 Is 66:12

Chapter Four
 1 Jn 15:11
 2 Rm 14:17
 3 Mt 5:1
 4 Ep 1:3–6
 5 Rm 8:9
 6 Lk 4:18; Mt 3:16
 7 Jn 16:13
 8 Jn 14:26
 9 Mt 23:10
10 Jn 6:68
11 Mt 5:13
12 1 Co 2:2
13 Jn 16:6
14 Jn 8:12
15 Jn 15:8
16 Jn 3:36
17 Jn 8:38
18 Jn 7:16
19 Ps 34:8
20 Ps 41:1 (LXX)
21 Ps 112:1
22 Rm 14:17
23 Ga 5:22
24 Lk 1:44

25 Jn 3:29
26 Jn 15:11
27 Jn 16:22
28 1 Jn 1:3
29 Si 30:16
31 Si 1:11
32 Si 1:18
33 Is 12:1–3
34 Rv 21:4
35 Mt 5:12
36 Is 61:10

Chapter Five
 1 Ga 2:19
 2 1 Co 1:23
 3 Lk 9:23
 4 Heb 10:5–7
 5 Jn 10:18
 6 Heb 12:2
 7 Heb 10:10,
   cf. 1 P 2:21–25
 8 Mt 10:24
 9 1 P 2:20–21
10 Ga 2:19–20
11 Col 1:24
12 Rituale
13 Rituale
14 Heb 12:3
15 Mt 11:28
16 Mt 26:31
17 Lk 22:32
18 Rule, ch. I
19 Consuetudines Cartusiae,
   c.16
20 Ps 56:8

Chapter Six
 1 Is 35:1–2
 2 Jr 2:7
 3 Sg 7:5
 4 Is 35:2
 5 Is 33:9
 6 Am 1:2
 7 Na 1:4
 8 Is 35:2
 9 I K 18:41–45
10 I K 17:3–4
11 I K 18:20–40
12 1 K 18:41–46
13 Sg 5:2
14 Ps 29:8
15 St Gregory
   Nazianzen
16 Ps 74:21
17 Ps 68:6
18 Rv 3:20
19 Ps 119:18
21 Ps 119:37
22 Mt 6:6
23 Ps 38:9
24 Ps 42:1–2
25 I K 17:3–4
26 Lk 1:78
27 Sg 11:14
28 Ps 36:8–9
29 Is 43:19
30 Is 41:18–19
31 Is 35:1–2
32 Is 35:6–7

Part Three: The Temple

1 Ps 48:9
2 Col 3:3
3 Ps 65:4
4 Rv 7:15–17

Chapter One
1 Gn 1:31
2 Canticle, v.5.
3 Jb 38:7
4 Ibid. 8
5 Ibid. 9
6 Ibid.12
7 Ibid. 24
8 Ibid. 38
9 St John of the Cross
10 Gn 1:31
11 Ws 11:24
12 Ps 145:9
13 Ps 96:6
14 Gn 3:8
15 Ws 11:25
16 St John of the Cross
17 Ps 19
18 Sermon on the Worship of God
19 Dn 3:57
20 Ps 19:1–4
21 Ps 104:4
22 Ps 104:13–14 (LXX)
23 Ps 145:16
24 Ps 18:9–11; 104:1–3
25 Lk 12:27–28
26 Lk 7:24
28 Mt 16:2
29 Jn 4:35
30 Mt 7:13–14

31 Mt 24:27
32 Jn 1:5; 8:12; 12:35–36f
33 Mt 23:37
34 Mt 6:26
35 Mt 10:16
36 Jn 10
37 Jn 4:13; 7:38
38 Jn 8:12
39 Jn 14:6
40 Jn 6:35
41 Mt 21:42
42 Jn 10:7
43 Sg 2:1
44 Ws 7:26
45 Heb 1:3
46 St John of the Cross
47 Rabindranath Tagore
48 The Curé d'Ars
49 Lacordaire
50 Gustave Thibon
51 Jn 14:27
52 John Henry Newman
53 St Gregory Nazianzen
54 Marie-Noel
55 Ps 18:36
56 Ps 6:2
57 Rv 12:1
58 Gn 2:15
59 Jr 2:21
60 Is 5:4
61 Mt 24:32
62 Sg 2:1
63 Sg 4:12
64 Sg 5:1
65 The Centurion's Journey,5
66 Ps 150:1, 6.

Chapter Two

1 Ps 122:1–2
2 1 K 6
3 Ex 40:34–35
4 2 Ch 5:14
5 Ps 84:10
6 Ps 122:1; 42:3–4
7 Ex 28; Lv 16; Heb 7
8 Jn 11:28
9 Mt 23:10
10 Jn 6:68
11 Lk 20:21
12 Jn 14:6
13 Lk 9–35
14 Mt 4:23
15 Mt 9:20; 14:36
16 Te Deum
17 1 Tm 2:5
18 Ch.4
19 Ho 2:16–22
20 1 Co 11:26
21 Rm 5:10
22 Rm 6:5
23 Ps 119:116
24 Ga 2:20
25 Ph 2:5
26 1 Ch 29:17
27 Ps 122:1–2
28 Ps 122:8–9

Chapter Three

1 Lk 6:12
2 Col 2:9
3 Canon of the Mass
4 Jn 15:14
5 Jn 15:15
6 Jn 4:31
7 Jn 4:6

8 Mt 8:24
9 Lk 19:41
10 Mt 26:40–43
11 Mt 19:13–15; 18:2–9
12 Lk 5:8
13 Mt 16:16
14 Jn 13:24–25
15 1 Jn 1:1
16 Jn 2:19
17 Canon of the Mass
18 Jn 1:14
19 Mt 21:42–44; 1 P 2:4
20 Jn 2:37–39
21 Lk 10:25–37
22 Jn 8:26
23 Mt 5:17
24 Jn 14
25 Heb 10:5
26 Jn 14:6
27 Heb 10:19–20
28 Jn 4:23
29 Mk 1:35
30 Lk 5:16
31 Mt 14:23
32 Lk 6:12
33 Jn 17:3
34 Jn 17:4
35 Jn 17:25
36 Jn 17:26
37 Jn 17:11
38 Jn 17:24
39 Jn 16:28
40 Jn 1:8
41 Jn 17:21
42 Jn 14:10–11
43 Mt 3:17; 17:5
44 Jn 16:28
45 Jn 15:5

46 Jn 17:2
47 Jn 18:37
48 Jn 17:10
49 Jn 16:7
40 Jn 17:24
51 Jn 5:20
52 Jn 14:28
53 Lk 10:21
54 Ph 2:7
55 Heb 10:7
56 Heb 10:10
57 Ph 2:7
58 Ph 2:8
59 Jn 4:34
60 Lk 12:50
61 Jn 17:11
62 Jn 17:13
63 1 Tm 2:5
64 Jn 16:23–24
65 Heb 5:7
66 Te Deum

Chapter Four
1 Lk 1:35
2 Sg 8:5
3 Lk 1:38
4 Mt 2:11
5 Ps 73:25
6 Ps 46:5
7 Ps 87:2 (LXX)
8 Ps 132:13–14
9 Ps 68:16
10 1 Co 3:16
11 2 Co 6:19
12 Is 55:1. Mass of Mary
   Mediatrix
13 Lk 1:46–47
14 Lk 1:49

15 Lk 1:48
16 Lk 1:38
17 1 Co 7:22; Rm 6:32
18 Heb 10:7
19 Ph 2:7; Mt 20:28
20 Ps 123:1–2
21 Rm 11:33
22 Is 55:8
23 Lk 9:23
24 Rm 8:32
25 Jn 15:1–2
26 Jn 12:24
27 Ps 126:5–6
28 Ep 1:17
29 1 Co 1:25
30 Sg 6:3
31 Si 24:30–31 (Vulg.)

Chapter Five
1 1 P 2:5
2 Col 2:9
3 Ep 5:30; 1:22–23, cf.
   Col 1:18
4 Ep 5:26–27
5 Ep 5:29
6 Rituale
7 Rm 12:5
8 1 Co 12:26
9 1 Co 10:17
10 Ep 4:13
11 1 P 2:5
12 Cf. Rm 12:6–8; 1 Co 12
13 Col 2:19; Ep 4:16
14 2 Pet 2:5
15 Ibid, 9
16 Heb 13:15
17 Col 1:24
18 Ep 5:24

19 v.27
20 Sg 2:14
21 Sg 8:13
22 Michel Carouges
23 St John of the Cross
24 Bull Umbratilem
25 Mk 8:36
26 Ep 4:16
27 Col 2:19
28 Ep 4:16
29 1 Co 10:16–17
30 Rm 12:1
31 Col 1:24

Chapter Six
 1 1 Co 6:20
 2 1 Co 3:16:17
 3 1 Co 6:19–20
 4 Rituale
 5 Cf. Rm 5:5
 6 Jn 14:23
 7 Jn 17:3
 8 1 Co 3:16
 9 Ep 2:19
10 1 Co 6:19

11 Hymn for the Dedication
    of a Church
12 1 Co 6:19
13 Ps 2:7
14 Ps 2:7
15 Jn 1:18
16 Fr de Régnon: Studies in
    Theology: Posit. Trinit.
    I:II
17 1 Jn 3:1; Ga 4:4
18 Jn 17:24
19 Jn 1:18
20 Cf. Jn 17:20–24
21 Ps 42:1–2
22 Rv 3:20
23 Cf. Ga 4:6
24 Rm 8:26–27
25 Cf. Mt 6:6
26 Heb 7:25
27 Rv 5:11–14

Epilogue
 1 Sg 2:4
 2 Sg 2:4